Central Government for Journalists

Central Government for Journalists

Edited by John Alexander

This book has been compiled by members of the Public Administration Board of the National Council for the Training of Journalists.

Contributors

David Kett
David English
George Harding
David Sanders

Edited by John Alexander

© LGC Communications and NCTJ
ISBN 0 904677 33 8

First published August 1988
Second Impression May 1990
Published by LGC Communications
122, Minories, London, EC3N 1NT.
Tel: 071-623 2530

Printed by Carlton Barclay Ltd, Southend, Essex

A CRUCIAL SUBJECT

Since the early 1950s, newspaper journalists have been formally trained and examined under an industry-wide scheme master-minded by the NCTJ.

It all started after publication of the 1949 report of the Royal Commission on the Press.

Basic training is almost exclusively carried out in the provincial newspaper field. Many reporters and sub-editors later go on to join national newspapers or enter other branches of journalism.

From the outset, they need to learn about government. In one form or another, it is at the centre of (and certainly relevant to) probably half of the thousands of news items which appear in papers all over the UK every week.

The NCTJ's Public Administration Board devises the Council's syllabuses and sets its exams. Now the Board has produced this excellent new text book to cover the range of central government knowledge that all journalists need to acquire.

The Council is grateful to the Board members and hopes that the book will be an invaluable aid to trainees all over the country.

KEITH HALL
Director,
National Council for the
Training of Journalists

4

CONTENTS

NATIONAL COUNCIL FOR THE TRAINING OF JOURNALISTS

Public Administration Syllabus

CENTRAL GOVERNMENT

ROLE OF THE EXECUTIVE (*in outline*). To include the Monarchy (Royal Prerogative), Prime Minister, Cabinet (collective responsibility), Ministers (ministerial responsibility, including delegated legislation and circulars). The role of the Civil Service.

ROLE OF THE LEGISLATURE (*in outline*). House of Commons, House of Lords, legislative process (1st, 2nd, 3rd reading, committee and report stage), Private Members' Bills, Private Bills, Question Time, Debate on the Adjournment, party discipline (Whips), role of the MP, relationship with the EEC.

POLITICS (*in outline*). Parliamentary election procedure, organisation of the political parties (e.g. NEC, Executive Committee, party conference).

CENTRAL GOVERNMENT SERVICES. A broad picture, with particular reference to the following:

(a) SOCIAL SERVICES: Department of Health and Social Security — National Insurance and Supplementary Benefits (organisation and benefits available) and Supplementary Benefits Commission, and Appeals Tribunal.

(b) NATIONAL HEALTH SERVICE: Organisation, finance and policy; membership of the various bodies, complaints procedure and role of the Health Service Commissioner.

(c) ENVIRONMENT AND TRANSPORT: The role of the Department of the Environment and its responsibility together with local government in urban and rural protection and pollution. The role of the Department of Transport.

(d) EMPLOYMENT AND INDUSTRY: Economic Planning and Aid to Industry — physical controls and inducements (e.g. location of industry, financial aid); Safety at work (Health and Safety Commission); Department of Employment (Manpower Services Commission); Advisory, Conciliation and Arbitration Service.

(e) HOME OFFICE: Prisons, parole boards, aliens, immigrants, broadcasting, powers of the Home Secretary. Its role together with local government in relation to the police service.

NATIONALISED INDUSTRIES AND PUBLIC UTILITIES (*in outline*).

EUROPEAN COMMUNITY.

CURRENT DEVELOPMENTS AFFECTING CENTRAL GOVERNMENT.

Preface

The Public Administration Board has long been conscious of the lack of a suitable text book on central government which meets the needs of the NCTJ syllabus and the needs of journalists in training.

After much heart searching, the Board came to the conclusion that the quickest and most satisfactory way to fill the gap was to do the job itself. My thanks are due to those members of the Board who have given up a tremendous amount of time to undertake the task. We know there are shortcomings but these will be faced head on and improvements will be made in future issues.

So much is likely to change within the lifetime of the present government that, to get the book out without undue delay, we have had to decide to state things as they are at the time of writing, noting those areas where change is contemplated or projected and warning where change is likely.

We also felt there was some very useful material not actually covered in the present syllabus, but which would help trainees more readily understand the working of our governmental or economic system. This has been included as an appendix to this edition.

We are grateful to the National Council for their encouragement and to our publishers, LGC Communications, for all their help and guidance. We hope that, like the companion publication "Local Government for Journalists", this book will not only be invaluable to trainee journalists but prove to be a useful reference book in newspaper offices.

George Harding,
Chairman,
NCTJ Public Administration Board.

Eastbourne 1988

CHAPTER 1

THE CONSTITUTION AND MONARCHY

Outlines the basic elements of the constitution — legislature, executive and judiciary; also describes the role and powers of the Monarch.

If a country is to have any sort of order and harmony, then there must be rules governing people's relationships with each other.

In some states, such as the federal states of the U.S.A. and Australia, these rules (laws) are written down and become **The Constitution**. In Britain there is no written constitution, no rigid single document, which could not readily be amended.

Instead, effective government has been established in Britain over many years by adopting a very flexible system relying on a number of sources, including convention and treatises.

Much of Britain's constitution is written in statutes and in the standing orders of both Houses of Parliament but, unlike countries with rigid constitutions, anything on paper can be changed if it is the will of Parliament.

Few, however, would challenge the two fundamental aims of our system:-

● Choice by the people of a government which has effective power to carry out their wishes

● Ultimate control kept in the hands of the electors, who are able to change the government at least once in five years.

That having been established, there are three types of activity which must be carried out in any constitution:-

Making of laws - the **LEGISLATURE** (the Queen in Parliament)

Executing of laws - the **EXECUTIVE** (the Prime Minister and Government)

Adjudicating in disputes - the **JUDICIARY** (the legal system).

Before dealing with these in more detail, it is valuable to recognise the many sources of the British Constitution.

SOURCES OF THE CONSTITUTION

Statutes

These have laid down basic rights and principles which form the basis for many laws. For example:-

1215 Magna Carta. The King agreed not to impose feudal tax without consent of the Common Council of the Realm

1628 Petition of Right. Established the principle of no taxation without the consent of Parliament, and no imprisonment of a person without lawful cause

1911 and 1949 Parliament Act. Limited the delaying powers of the House of Lords over the Commons

1968 Race Relations Act. Prohibited prejudice on the grounds of race, colour or ethnic origin

1969 Representation of the People Act. Reduced the voting age to 18.

Case Law

These are pronouncements made by judges in dealing with specific cases. When followed and applied by succeeding judges and magistrates they become an important source of constitutional law:-

1936 Thomas v Sawkins: The police are entitled to enter a public meeting if they have reasonable suspicion that a breach of the peace is likely to occur

1947 Christie v Leachinsky: A person arrested by the police must be informed of the charge or crime of which he is suspected.

Conventions

Conventions are the rules of political practice. They are not laws, and cannot be enforced as such. Typical conventions are:-

The Cabinet operates according to the wishes of the Prime Minister. No law dictates how government should work

The Prime Minister is chosen from the largest party

Ministers must exercise collective responsibility

The Queen must act on Cabinet advice

In cases of conflict between the two Houses, the Lords shall yield to the Commons.

Political conventions are based on customs and practice, their real sanction being political opinion.

Treatises

Political philosophers and thinkers affect public opinion, initiating new ideas on legislation. Montesquieu (1689-1755) saw the strength of British government being the separation of powers between the Legislature, the Executive and the Judiciary. In his view, this avoided misgovernment and a drift towards dictatorship. Other famous writers include John Locke, Blackstone, Edmund Burke, J.S. Mill, A.V. Dicey and Erskine May, whose Parliamentary Practice is used to regulate Commons' procedure today.

PRINCIPLES OF THE CONSTITUTION

Democracy

Britain is said to be a democracy (or more accurately, an indirect democracy). This is a term used to describe a political system which accepts certain basic assumptions:-

> Government should reflect the people's will and be answerable to the electorate ("Government of the people, for the people, by the people")
>
> The law should be applied equally to all
>
> There should be an independent Judiciary and an Executive which is separately elected and responsible to an elected legislature.

The Separation of Powers

To a degree, the three powers are separated but there is an overlap:-

> The Queen is head of the Executive and Judiciary and is an integral part of the Legislature
>
> The Lord Chancellor is a member of Cabinet, presides over the House of Lords and is head of the Judiciary under the Crown
>
> The Cabinet inevitably includes the overlap of Legislature and Executive
>
> The Lords is part of the Legislature and also the final legal Court of Appeal
>
> The Judiciary shapes the law by its rulings.

Parliamentary Sovereignty

This is a legal doctrine, recognised by the courts, which lays down that Parliament can pass and repeal any law it likes. Britain's membership both of the EC and NATO in fact call into question the strict interpretation of this doctrine.

Political Sovereignty

The legal sovereignty of Parliament is only tolerated because of the political sovereignty of the electorate. Elections have to be held every five years, thus ensuring that Parliament is subject to the wishes of all adults over the age of 18 having a right to vote. A government no longer having the trust or support of the majority of British people would thus be voted out of office.

Rule of Law

Individual liberty is said to be protected by the "rule of law" —the restriction of government action to that authorised by law. The nineteenth century academic Professor A.V. Dicey articulated this doctrine. He established that to make government acceptable, the constitution must provide the individual with guarantees against the disorder of anarchy and the oppression of tyranny.

THE ROLE OF THE MONARCHY

Britain has a constitutional Monarchy. "The Queen reigns, but does not rule," is the best summary. She is the personification of the state.

Walter Bagehot saw the Monarch as having three rights. The right to be consulted, the right to encourage and the right to warn. The Prime Minister has an audience with the Queen once a week, usually on a Tuesday afternoon. On these occasions the Prime Minister will advise on legislative plans and developments, and the Queen will offer observations drawn from her reading and experience over 35 years.

Harold Wilson is so far the only modern Prime Minister to have written about such meetings with the Queen. His memoirs make it clear that the Queen can bring a non-partisan dimension to discussions.

Her main functions are:-

Queen's Speech

The Queen's Speech at the opening of each session of Parliament is written by the Government and lays down legislative policy for the ensuing Parliament.

Dissolving, Proroguing and Summoning Parliament

Under the Parliament Acts of 1911 and 1949, Parliament is dissolved at the end of a five-year period, unless the Prime Minister asks for an earlier dissolution or is defeated in a motion of "No Confidence" in the House. Constitutionally, the Monarch cannot refuse a **dissolution** request.

Prorogation is the closing of a session of both Houses of Parliament. A session usually lasts from November to November. Prorogation terminates all public business. Any public bills, except those going through under the Parliament Acts, lapse if they have not completed all stages in both Houses.

Appointing the Prime Minister

The Prime Minister is appointed by the Monarchy by right of the royal prerogative, but the appointment is very much bound by convention. If there is a party in the House with a majority and a recognised leader, then the Monarchy must invite that leader to be the Prime Minister.

If the Government is defeated in the House and the Prime Minister resigns, the Monarch may consult the leader of the Opposition and others to see if an alternative government can be formed. Usually, the Opposition Leader cannot do this because of lack of a parliamentary majority and the Monarch must call a General Election.

The Queen's real influence comes in the event of a hung Parliament. The usual procedure is to consult with Privy Councillors before deciding who to invite to form a government or coalition.

All cabinet ministers and other senior ministers as well as senior opposition figures are members of the **Privy Council**. They are formally appointed by the Sovereign and may be removed at will (though they seldom are). They take an oath of office, binding themselves to "keep the Queen's council secret". Members are addressed as "Right Honourable" and have precedence in Parliamentary debate. There are currently around 400 such Privy Councillors.

The Privy Council only meets in full on the death of the Monarch and in practice only a handful of members are required to attend for most of its functions. The role of the Privy Council is to make certain Crown appointments, issue Royal Charters to Boroughs and Universities, and to issue Orders in Council (see delegated legislation).

A committee of the Privy Council, known as the Judicial Committee, made up of judicial members hears appeals from some Commonwealth countries, courts of the Isle of Man, Channel Islands and some tribunals.

Fountain of Justice

The courts of law are Royal Courts, with justice being administered by Her Majesty's Judges who are appointed by the Crown. All prosecutions take place in the Royal name (e.g. Regina v..........). By prerogative, the Queen can remit all or part of any sentence or penalty on a person convicted of crime. But she would act only on the advice of the Home Secretary after a thorough investigation of a case.

Fountain of Honour

The Monarch confers peerages, baronetcies, knighthoods and other honours including the CBE and OBE. Traditionally, these appear in the **Honours Lists**, of which there are three:-

New Year's Honours

Birthday Honours (published on the Queen's birthday)

Resignation or Dissolution Honours.

Technically, she also appoints officers in the Armed Forces, Governors of Commonwealth countries, diplomats and senior positions in the established Church. But again, most of these are subject to the advice of the Prime Minister. There are a few ceremonial honours which are entirely within the Monarch's gift, namely the Order of Merit, the Royal Victorian Order, the Most Noble Order of the Garter and the Most Noble and Most Ancient Order of the Thistle.

Head of Commonwealth

The Queen is head of the Commonwealth and has the same powers of advice and influence in its governmental affairs as she does in Britain.

In Commonwealth countries she is represented by a Governor General, and by a Governor in dependencies, which are not members of the Commonwealth. In the Channel Islands and the Isle of Man, she is represented by a Lieutenant Governor.

Formal and ceremonial

The Monarch also undertakes formal and ceremonial functions, such as the State Opening of Parliament, and the Trooping of the Colour as well as entertaining visiting Heads of State.

The Civil List

The Civil List covers the personal income of the Sovereign, plus expenses of the Royal Household and an allowance made by Parliament for other members of the Royal Family. It is covered in the 1952 Civil List Act. The Queen is exempt from taxes. In return for this support, revenue from the sale of royal land and properties reverts to the Treasury. Prince Charles is known to want to end the Civil List payment, replacing it instead with income from Crown lands direct to the Monarchy.

CHAPTER 2

THE LEGISLATURE

Outlines the functions of the House of Commons and the House of Lords; describes the role of an MP and the Opposition.

The British Parliament has three elements, the Monarch, The House of Lords and the House of Commons. Because legislation has to pass through two chambers for discussion and debate, Britain is said to have a bi-cameral legislature.

HOUSE OF COMMONS

Britain has 650 Members of Parliament who represent constituencies each containing around 60,000 to 70,000 electors. The maximum life of a government is five years, though the Prime Minister may call an election at any time within that period. But it would be necessary to hold a general election if the Government lost a 'No Confidence' vote, as happened to James Callaghan's Labour Government in 1979.

The role of the Commons is to scrutinise legislation proposed by the Executive, then to pass, amend or veto it. No goverment would last long if its proposals were constantly rejected.

ROLE OF BACKBENCH MPs

A **backbench** MP is a member of the Commons who is not a member of the government or shadow cabinet. Backbenchers are seen to have four main obligations.

To the nation as a whole

The MP is expected to approach legislation from the point of view of Britain as a whole, giving consideration to the national good rather than regional or sectional interests.

To his conscience

There are several issues recognised in Parliament where MPs are allowed a free vote rather than having to follow a whip. This is where members feel strongly on issues which often cut across party politics.

Examples of conscience votes are Sidney Silverman's private member's bill to abolish hanging and David Steel's bill to allow abortion in certain circumstances. Where an MP feels sufficiently strongly on an issue of conscience, he may sometimes break the party whip. A recent example was a Conservative backbenchers' revolt against Government plans to introduce Sunday trading.

To his constituency

The MP has a duty to represent all his constituents, even those who voted against him in the election. He must be vigilant to ensure government legislation does not pose a threat either to the jobs or welfare of the people he represents or to the environment in his constituency.

To his party

The MP is expected to support his party's manifesto. The party has funded his election campaign (many Labour MPs are sponsored by trades unions) and provided workers to ensure he is elected. The MP is, therefore, expected to return that help by showing loyalty and commitment to ensure his party's policies are supported in Parliament. In the Conservative Party, this support is perhaps more implicit than in the Labour Party, where there can be more explicit pressure on a member through the General Management Committee of his constituency party.

In Parliament, discipline rests with the whips and all MPs receive notice of business in the House for the coming week. If three lines appear under any item then the Member knows his absence from the vote will be excused for only the most exceptional of reasons (hence the three-line whip).

'Pairing' with a Member in the opposite party (where two members of opposing parties agree not to vote) is permitted with the approval of the Whips' Office. All the party leaders appoint whips in their own parties to act as a link between the leadership and the backbenchers in order to ensure that both sides are aware of each others' views and that the backbenchers vote according to the wish of the leadership.

THE HOUSE OF COMMONS AT WORK

Schedule

The Commons meets in four periods — November to Christmas, January to Easter, Easter to Whitsun and Whitsun to July.

On Monday to Thursday, the House sits from 2.30pm to 10.30pm but if the business is important or urgent, the sitting can sometimes continue all night.

On Fridays the House meets from 9.30am to 3pm, finishing early to allow MPs to return to their constituencies for weekend engagements.

The Speaker

The Commons is chaired by Mr. Speaker, a member appointed by his fellows. His political allegiance immediately ceases on taking office and his role is to control debate and enforce rules as well as to act as the mouthpiece of the Commons in its relations with the Crown and the Lords.

Once appointed, a Speaker continues in office until he decides to retire. In a General Election, he stands in his constituency as "Mr. Speaker seeking re-election".

His other powers are:—

Certifying whether a bill is a Money Bill. This is a bill dealing with the raising of finance

Executing the orders of the House

Signing warrants for the issuing of writs for by-elections

Issuing warrants for committal for contempt of the House and for witnesses to attend to give evidence

Issuing reprimands to Members or members of the public (strangers) for breach of privilege

Supervising and controlling all departments of the House of Commons.

Parliamentary Privilege

Members of Parliament enjoy rights and privileges which are enshrined in common law. These rights allow members to do their duty. The main privileges are freedom from arrest and freedom of speech and debate, within the precincts of Parliament, and the right of access to the Queen. Parliament has the right to regulate its own proceedings (e.g. suspending a member), right to regulate its own composition and power to punish for breach of privilege or contempt.

The Leader of the House of Commons

The Leader of the House is the member of government primarily responsible for organising the business of the House and for providing reasonable facilities for the House to debate matters about which it is concerned. An important role is to announce each week's programme of business in the Commons and to act as spokesman for the House, in the PM's absence, on ceremonial and other occasions.

Role of the Opposition

The party with the second largest number of seats in the Commons is recognised as "Her Majesty's Opposition" (or "The Official Opposition"). Its leader receives an additional salary for occupying that post. Its role is to question and challenge the government, to keep it constantly accountable for the way in which it exercises its powers. It also presents itself as an alternative government at election time.

LEGISLATIVE PROCESS

Public and Private Bills

There are four types of bill:—

Public Bills — change the general law of the Land (e.g. 1944 Education Act, 1965 Race Relations Act). Bills can be introduced first into either House.

Private Members' Bills — are public bills introduced by a backbench MP who wins a top place in the ballot to introduce the bill on selected days, or who uses the Ten Minute Rule to seek to introduce a bill.

Private Bills — usually of a local character and most commonly presented by a local authority or a Port Authority.

Hybrid Bills — a cross between a public bill and a private bill (e.g. 1965 Severn Bridge Tolls Act).

Progress of a Bill

First Reading: The clerk of the House formally reads out the title of the bill and the Minister normally names the day for the Second Reading.

Second Reading: The general principles of the proposed bill are debated and voted upon in the Commons.

Committee Stage: The details of the bill are now scrutinised clause by clause usually by a standing committee or committee of the whole House.

The Report Stage: The Chairman formally reports back to the Commons with the amended bill. Further amendments may be made.

Third Reading: The bill is reviewed in its final form in a purely formal way. Verbal amendments may be taken.

"Another Place": The bill is then passed to the House of Lords for its consideration. Its progress is similar to that in the

Commons, except that the committee stage is usually of the Whole House. Under the Parliament Acts of 1911 and 1949, the Lords may only delay Commons' legislation, on which both sides do not agree, for up to one year.

Lords Report to the Commons: If amendments are made in the Lords and not accepted by the Commons, then a committee must be set up to seek to resolve the differences.

The Royal Assent: Before a bill can become law, it must gain the Royal Assent, which is read out in Norman French, "La Reine le Veult".

Delegated Legislation

Parliament in certain circumstances permits ministers, local authorities, public corporations and other statutory bodies to make laws. This is known as delegated legislation. The power to introduce such legislation and the procedure the minister must follow is laid down in Acts of Parliament.

Delegated legislation may be passed in three main ways:—

Order in Council	— the minister drafts the law and it is confirmed by the Monarch in the Privy Council
Statutory Instrument	— the minister drafts the law and it is laid before Parliament which may be asked to vote in favour or against before it becomes law
Bylaw	— local authorities, public corporations and statutory bodies may make bylaws which require ministerial approval.

Some 2,000 rules and regulations come into force each year through delegated legislation. MPs have little say over such legislation, though a Select Committee on Statutory Instruments reviews such laws.

PARLIAMENTARY COMMITTEES

There are five sorts:—

Standing Committees: Each session, the Commons appoints standing committees, which examine the details of a bill assigned to them. They consist of a chairman, plus no fewer than 20 and not more than 50 members, who are appointed on a basis of interests and experience but in proportion to party strengths.

There is also a *Scottish Standing Committee*, which has 30 Scottish MPs and up to 20 others. Its role is to scrutinise general legislation affecting Scotland as well as all financial matters. The *Welsh Grand Committee* is made up of the 36 Welsh MPs plus five other nominated members. It has similar powers to the Scottish committee.

Committee of the Whole House: For money bills and bills of special importance the examination stage may be taken by a committee of the Whole House. The House is presided over by **Chairman of Ways and Means**, effectively a Deputy Speaker.

Select Committees: Usually composed of 12 members, these are set up for three main purposes:

Supervision of Government administration, overseeing the operation and spending of a department. The committee can call Ministers, civil servants and heads of nationalised industries to give evidence. Since 1980, Select Committees oversee the following departments: Agriculture, Defence, Education, Employment, Environment, Foreign Affairs, Home Affairs, Trade and Industry, Social Services, Transport, the Military and the Civil Service.

To investigate specific matters. An example is the Ad Hoc committee set up in 1971 to look at the funding of the Royal Family.

To manage the House of Commons efficiently. These domestic committees are usually set up as and when they are needed.

Joint Committees. These are made up jointly of members of the Commons and Lords to deal with non-political matters and bills which deal with ratification or consolidation of a point of law.

Committees on Private Bills

Where such a bill is opposed, four MPs are appointed to examine it and report back to the Commons. If there is agreement the bill follows more or less the same procedure as a public bill.

FILIBUSTERING

The Government, in seeking to stick to its legislative time-table, often comes up against delaying tactics by opposition MPs. There are three methods open to them to stop filibustering or delaying matters in committee:—

> **Ordinary Closure** — at any stage of discussion, a member may move that "The question be now put". The matter is then voted upon and the next clause is debated.

> **The Kangaroo** — this is where the Government selects clauses to be discussed by the committee within the timetable set aside for discussion. Other clauses are not debated at all. Usually, every other clause is discussed. The other clauses are 'hopped over'.

> **Guillotine Closure** — this is where the Government sets a timetable for debate, forcing the Opposition to divide discussion time carefully in order to debate important clauses.

PRESENT COMPOSITION OF THE HOUSE OF COMMONS

ENGLAND	:	523 members
WALES	:	38 members
SCOTLAND	:	72 members
NORTHERN IRELAND	:	17 members

State of the Parties in the Commons after the 1987 General Election

Conservative	:	375
Labour	:	229
Liberal	:	17
SDP	:	5
SNP	:	3
Plaid Cymru	:	3

24

Ulster Unionist	:	9
Democratic Unionist	:	3
SDLP	:	3
Ulster Popular Unionist	:	1
Provisional Sinn Fein	:	1
Speaker	:	1
Total	:	650

THE INFLUENCE OF BACKBENCH MPs

Backbench MPs are not just "lobby fodder" as some people suppose, but can and do exert influence over the Executive in a number of ways:—

Question Time. Oral or written questions can be put to appropriate Ministers who must face the House and answer questions on a rota basis. Prime Minister's questions are on Tuesdays and Thursdays, when the political issues of the moment are usually well ventilated.

Ten Minute Rule and Adjournment Debate. Under the Ten Minute Rule, the member may speak for ten minutes on an issue about which he feels strongly and may seek to introduce legislation. Ten minutes is then allowed for a reply, after which the bill is voted upon.

The daily motion for adjournment at 10pm is another occasion when a member can win a precious half hour to debate a topic about which he feels strongly. The aim is to influence government policy.

Private Members' Bills

Time is set aside on a Friday for debate on Private Members' bills. Members enter a ballot for places to introduce legislation. Only a very small number have any chance of success.

Robin Squire's Local Government (Access to Information) Act of 1985, affecting access to local government meetings, is an often quoted example of a successful Private Members' Bill.

Other ways in which backbenchers can have some influence is through membership of Standing and Select Committees, through debate on the floor of the House of Commons and through the force of their backbench groupings.

The Conservative **1922 Committee** and the **Parliamentary Labour Party** are backbench lobby groups which their party leaderships have to take seriously in order to ensure support in the House.

HOUSE OF LORDS

The House of Lords is composed of four main groups:—

Hereditary Peers. These are peers who have inherited their title. There are some 750 hereditary peers of the UK and Scotland but about a third of these have applied for leave of absence and a handful have disclaimed their titles to follow political ambitions in the House of Commons. Three famous cases come to mind: Tony Benn (formerly Lord Stansgate), Sir Alec Douglas-Home (Lord Home) and Quintin Hogg (Lord Hailsham).

Life Peers. These are created under the Life Peerage Act of 1958 and are usually seen as rewards for years of political work in the Commons or for exceptional endeavour in other walks of life.

Lords Spiritual. Twenty-six Lords hold office by virtue of being bishops of the established Church of England. The Archbishops of Canterbury and York, and the Bishops of Durham, London and Winchester have seats as of right. The other 21 take office as senior diocesan bishops, based on their length of service.

Lords of Appeal. Often referred to as the Law Lords. There are 19, who perform the judicial work of the House when it sits as a final Court of Appeal.

The House of Lords considers bills (apart from money bills) sent up from the Commons and can either reject or amend a bill. The Commons never has enough time to consider all aspects of new legislation so the Lords takes on a "tidying up" role.

Amendments are intended to improve a bill but if they are not accepted by the Commons, the Lords usually give way.

Bills can be introduced in the Lords but by convention they are seldom controversial. As most Life Peers are specialists in their subject debates in the Lords are, as a rule, of a very high standard.

As well as its deliberation function, the Lords also has an important judicial function. It is the supreme and final court of appeal in the UK.

The House is presided over by the **Lord Chancellor** (also a Member of the Cabinet) who sits on the Woolsack, the red covered wool-upholstered seat in front of the Throne.

Is a Second Chamber necessary?

Because the Lords can reject a non-money bill, demands for its abolition or reform are a frequent occurrence.

Those who are against the House of Lords say it is unrepresentative, that unelected members are there more often by accident of birth, and they are drawn from an unrepresentative section of society.

A large in-built Conservative bias can impede the progress of a democratically elected left wing government and this is also a cause of irritation when the Conservatives do not control the Commons. But since 1979 there have been as many amendments introduced by the Lords as by the Commons.

Another inconsistency is that hereditary peers do not attend, or attend only for specific debates when they are whipped in.

Those who wish to see the Lords preserved regard it as a safeguard against a government which may want to meddle with the constitution or push through Parliament radical measures not in its election programme. Rejection by the Lords at least allows time for reflection and public reaction.

Most people in public life view the Lords as a place where there is time for more reflective debate and discussion away from the party political heat of the Commons, a place where specialists can initiate discussion on non-political issues and a place where men and women of standing can look at topics on a much broader national dimension.

The House of Lords 1987

Peers of the Royal Blood	:	4
Archbishops	:	2
Dukes	:	25
Marquesses	:	28
Earls and Countesses	:	157
Viscounts	:	103
Bishops	:	24
Barons and Baronesses	:	845, of whom 365 are Life Peers

Hansard

Hansard is the official report of deliberations in the House of Commons and House of Lords. This records answers to all parliamentary questioning and reports debates, verbatim. Hansard has absolute privilege but when quoted only qualified privilege.

The Parliamentary Commissioner for Administration

The Commissioner or Ombudsman was first appointed in 1966 to investigate complaints of injustice or maladministration brought against the implementation of central government policies. These complaints have to be brought to his attention by an MP on behalf of a constituent and he makes his report to Parliament.

The Act appointing the Commissioner defined maladministration as bias, neglect, inattention, delay, incompetence, ineptitude, perversity, turpitude, and arbitrariness — or any situation in which a civil servant's action had been improper or seriously inadequate. He can reach three conclusions:—

Maladministration with injustice

Maladministration without injustice

No maladministration.

He can investigate Government departments, the Public Records Office, the Registry of Friendly Societies, the Royal Mint and any other body set up to carry out functions on behalf of the Crown.

CHAPTER 3

THE EXECUTIVE

Powers of the Prime Minister, checks on those powers and the relationship of PM to Cabinet. Summarises the role of Civil Servants and their relationship with Ministers.

The role of the Executive is to formulate policy and then ensure its implementation after it has been passed by Parliament. The main thrust of policy formation comes from the Prime Minister and the Cabinet.

THE PRIME MINISTER

The Prime Minister is now acknowledged as being the person who is head of the majority party in the Commons, though in a hung Parliament the Monarch may exercise discretion in deciding who she invites to form the Government. The first Prime Minister is accepted as being Sir Robert Walpole, who headed the Government from 1721 to 1742.

No salary is attached to the post of Prime Minister. Instead, the salary is determined by whatever other posts the person holds. Mrs. Thatcher's salary comes from her title as **First Lord of the Treasury** and Minister for the Civil Service. Her official residence is 10, Downing Street, and she also has the use of Chequers, a country house in Buckinghamshire.

Powers of the Prime Minister

The Prime Minister is leader of the majority party in Parliament and head of the Government. In this capacity she can:—

Select Cabinet ministers

Appoint other members of the Government

Reshuffle ministers as she thinks appropriate

Dismiss ministers or ask them to resign

Chair the Cabinet and several Cabinet committees

Co-ordinate policy and supervise the activities of departments to ensure corporate management

Act as the nation's chief spokesman in national and international affairs

Appoint Government whips who will ensure party discipline

Exercise patronage through the appointment of offices, judicial and ecclesiastical, and the dispensing of titles

Adopt powers of appointment and promotion as political head of the Civil Service

Act as the Government's main link with the Queen.

The powers are such that in his introduction to Bagehot's "The English Constitution", Richard Crossman, a minister in Harold Wilson's Labour Governments of the 1960's wrote: "The post war epoch has seen the final transformation of Cabinet Government into Prime Ministerial Government."

Constraints on the power of the Prime Minister

Backbenchers, through the **1922 Committee** of the Conservative Party, or the Parliamentary Labour Party, cannot always be taken for granted and can exert influence on the Prime Minister and Government.

The 1922 Committee is made up of all backbench Conservative MPs who meet once or twice a week during a Parliamentary session to discuss the business of the House and important matters of the moment. Cabinet ministers can be invited to address its members to seek support for controversial legislation.

Mrs. Thatcher had to abandon plans for Sunday trading in 1986/87 after her backbench MPs voted against the legislation. Backbenchers also forced the resignation of a Prime Ministerial favourite, Leon Brittan, during the Westland crisis, when Michael Heseltine also resigned.

Backbench pressures, via the whips, is also said to have prevented an early return to Government of the Prime Minister's trusted adviser Cecil Parkinson who had resigned over the Sarah Keays' affair.

The **Parliamentary Labour Party** is made up of backbench Labour MPs (those not having Shadow Cabinet office). They met once a week to discuss the business of the House or matters of national importance, and can invited members of the Shadow Cabinet to addresss them.

It is a very strong Prime Minister, indeed, who sees no necessity to balance different sections of the party in the Cabinet. Some figures are just too powerful and important to be excluded, or can be too dangerous to the Government as outspoken backbenchers. Peter Walker's political philosophy is alleged to have been at odds with Mrs. Thatcher's in several important areas but his standing and influence on the liberal wing of the party has ensured his retention as a senior figure in the Cabinet.

In times of new administrations in particular, the Prime Minister is constrained by those members who have previous cabinet experience and perceived talent, or by senior party figures who can name the department they would like to lead.

Although the Prime Minister can dismiss ministers, there is a limit to the amount of butchery other party members will accept. She must earn the support of colleagues and cannot compel it.

Because of the complexity of modern government, the Prime Minister must rely on the advice of her ministers and cabinet committees on specific departmental matters. Many decisions are formed after careful research and discussion by cabinet committees and think tanks. The PM cannot force through a policy which doesn't command majority support.

First Among Equals?

Most constitutional textbooks describe the Prime Minister as being "Primus Inter Pares" — first among equals. She certainly has important powers through her sole right of appointment to the Government after winning a general election.

Equally, there are constraints upon that power being absolute in a democratic society. Much depends on the personality of the Prime Minister.

Harold Wilson and Ted Heath were both consensus PMs, seeking to sum up Cabinet debate to reach a common view on policy issues. Mrs. Thatcher is much more an initiator and leader of Cabinet opinion, deciding what should be debated and seeking to promote policy and ideas.

As well as personality, much depends on the PM's standing both in the nation and the party. A PM enjoying national popularity is likely to be able to exert more influence on Cabinet than one struggling in the opinion polls as a credible national leader.

THE CABINET

The Cabinet, the composition of which is determined by the Prime Minister, will continue to flourish only if it commands the support of the majority of the members of Parliament in the legislature, the House of Commons. In 1988 there were 21 members. These were heads of major departments and ministers with specialist roles.

Positions

Prime Minister, First Lord of the Treasury and Minister of the Civil Service

Lord President of the Council

Secretary of State for Foreign and Commonwealth Affairs

Chancellor of the Exchequer

Lord Chancellor

Home Secretary

Secretary of State for Wales

Secretary of State for Defence

Secretary of State for Employment

Secretary of State for Northern Ireland

Secretary of State for the Environment

Secretary of State for Trade and Industry

Secretary of State for Education and Science

Chancellor of the Duchy of Lancaster and Minister for Trade and Industry

Minister of Agriculture, Fisheries and Food

Secretary of State for Scotland

Secretary of State for Transport

Secretary of State for Social Services

Secretary of State for Energy

Chief Secretary to the Treasury

Lord Privy Seal and Leader of the House of Lords

Leader of the House of Commons.

Walter Bagehot, writing "The English Constitution" in 1867, said of the importance of the Cabinet: "The efficient secret of the English Constitution may be described as the close union and nearly complete fusion of the executive and legislative powers. . . .

"The Cabinet is a combining committee — a hyphen which joins, a buckle which fastens the legislative part of the State to the executive power of the State. In its origin it belongs to one, in its function it belongs to the other."

The Cabinet's main characteristics can be listed as follows:—

No statutory basis, existing purely by convention

Operating on the principle of secrecy about its deliberations

Made up of MPs and peers of similar political views, who have usually been elected on a common political platform

Chosen from the party with a majority in the House of Commons

33

Selected by the Prime Minister, who is acknowledged to be its leader and chairman

Obliged to carry out a commonly agreed policy (the doctrine of collective responsibility means that ministers opposing the policy which commanded majority support must either resign or publicly support the majority view)

In the event of parliamentary censure, its members must resign collectively

The **Secretary of State** is the senior politician in charge of a government department. He will have Cabinet status. His deputies, who are not necessarily Cabinet members, are referred to as **Ministers of State** or **Parliamentary Under Secretaries**

Parliamentary Private Secretaries are MPs who are recruited by senior ministers to help them with liaison with fellow party MPs in the Commons.

Principles of Cabinet Government

The Cabinet must have the support of the Commons. The Cabinet must be able to have the support of the Legislature (Parliament) to pass its proposals. A government defeated in the Commons on a motion of confidence has to resign, as happened to James Callaghan's Labour Government in April, 1979.

Members of the Government must be of the same party or be members with an agreed common policy. Having fought a general election on an agreed manifesto, the role of the Government is to implement that manifesto.

It supports the doctrine of **collective responsibility** and offers unanimous advice to the Monarch, even when individual members have conflicting views. If a minister cannot agree with a policy, he should then resign.

This was cited by Michael Heseltine as the reason for his resignation from the Cabinet over the Westland affair in 1986. In 1938, Anthony Eden resigned as Foreign Secretary because he could not support the appeasement policy with Germany proposed by the Prime Minister, Neville Chamberlain. Aneurin Bevan and Harold Wilson resigned in 1951 when the Cabinet agreed to impose prescription charges for the first time.

34

Under the convention of **individual ministerial responsibility** a Secretary of State for a department, as ministerial head, is answerable for all its acts, and for its sins of omission. The Secretary of State must bear the consequences of any failure by his department which may be criticised by Parliament.

Such was the case in 1982 when Lord Carrington resigned as Foreign Secretary after Parliamentary criticism of his department's handling of the crisis in the Falkland Islands.

Servicing the Cabinet

The Cabinet Secretariat is made up of one Secretary, three Deputy Secretaries, four Under Secretaries and ten Assistant Secretaries. These are all Civil Servants. Their job is to prepare agendas, provide information on previous decisions of Cabinet, record decisions and notify departments where policy is affected. Cabinet meetings are now usually held once a week.

Cabinet Committees are set up on the instructions of the Prime Minister and in 1988 were:—

Defence Committee

Legislative Committee (considers draft legislation and supervises its passage through Parliament)

Future Legislation Committee (looks at ways of implementing future bills to be considered by Parliament)

Economic Committee

Home and Social Affairs Committee

Lord President's Committee (general purpose committee for items not falling into the domain of any other committee).

THE CIVIL SERVICE

Civil servants are full-time paid officials of the state who advise ministers on policy and then, after legislation has been passed by Parliament, ensure its implementation. There are three groups within the mainstream Civil Service, the Administrative Grade, Executive Grade and Clerical Grade.

Civil servants remain in post even when governments change, so it is important they are not seen to be party political.

Ministers have the help and support of **Permanent Secretaries** and **Private Secretaries**, paid civil servants who are there to give advice and guidance to the politician. Permanent Secretaries are the most senior civil servants and are responsible for the organisation and day-to-day running of their departments. They are also expected to advise ministers on legislation, assist in the preparation of speeches and be able to provide material and statistics to answer parliamentary questions.

They must not be confused with **Parliamentary Private Secretaries** who are unpaid MPs appointed to aid a Minister in the House of Commons at party political level.

Scotland and Wales are unusual in that they have their own civil service machinery, the Scottish and Welsh Offices.

The Scottish Office

In charge of the civil service is the **Secretary of State for Scotland** who is appointed by the Prime Minister. This is a Cabinet post. He is assisted by a Minister of State and three Parliamentary Under Secretaries of State.

The Scottish Office effectively encompasses five departments:

The Department of Agriculture and Fisheries for Scotland

The Scottish Development Department

The Scottish Education Department

The Scottish Home and Health Department

The Scottish Economic Planning Department.

Day-to-day administration is implemented by the Edinburgh office, but the Scottish Office itself is located in London.

The Scottish Law Officers are:

The Lord Advocate

The Solicitor-General for Scotland

The Welsh Office

The Welsh Office, based in Cardiff, is under the overall control of the **Secretary of State for Wales**, who is appointed by the Prime Minister. The appointment carries with it membership of the Cabinet.

The main functions undertaken by the department in Wales are:

Child care

Health

Housing

Local government control

Education

Town and country planning

Roads

Tourism

Agriculture (shared with the Minister of Agriculture, Fisheries and Food).

The Minister has general responsibility for Welsh economic developments and can give selective assistance to industry. In this, he is aided by the Welsh Development Agency.

The Secretary of State is aided by two Parliamentary Under Secretaries. The current Secretary of State is David Hunt.

CHAPTER 4

POLITICAL PARTIES AND PRESSURE GROUPS

Explains the organisation of the major political parties, including selection of candidates, and the role of pressure groups.

Political parties have three distinct levels of operation — at constituency level, within the central association and in a string-pulling capacity within the parliamentary party. There are fundamental differences between the Conservative Party and the Labour Party which reflect their different origins.

The Liberal Party has an anti-centralist approach in terms of hierarchy while the SDP, still struggling to solve its teething troubles, has not finally decided on how to order its affairs. Its instinct is to consult on most major issues on a one man, one vote basis.

THE CONSERVATIVE PARTY

The Conservative Party grew out of the Tory Party and evolved from a series of amalgamations with groups splitting from their main nineteenth century rivals, the Liberals.

Organisation

The basic unit around which the party operates is the **Constituency Association**, which is based on parliamentary divisions. It is run by an **executive council**, whose job it is to draw up a shortlist for the selection of a parliamentary candidate.

All members of the constituency association can attend the actual selection conference for the candidate, who must first have been approved by **Conservative Central Office**, the permanent headquarters of the party.

This is controlled by a **chairman** who is directly responsible to the leader of the party and appointed by her. Several constituencies are then linked together to form an area council, of which there are 12 for England and Wales.

The function of this unit is to co-ordinate the resources of the area and advise Central Office on organisational matters.

The **Central Council** is the national governing body of the party and is made up of a leader, officers of the party, Conservative MPs, all selected candidates for parliamentary seats and four representatives from each constituency association.

Because this unit is so large, with around 6,000 members, actual running of the party and research for policy lies in the hands of the **Executive Committee of the Central Council** which is made up of 150 members from the provincial Area Councils. It is further divided into sub-committees to deal with specific organisational issues.

National policy is debated at the **annual party conference**, usually held in the first week of October. Resolutions passed are not binding on the leader but are merely advisory.

Power lies effectively in the hands of the **leader** of the party who has to consult on the selection of the chairman of the party and whose selection can be influenced by other senior figures (e.g. Lord Whitelaw is alleged to have been against Lord Young's appointment as Party Chairman after Norman Tebbitt's resignation).

The Conservative Party leader is elected by a ballot of Conservative MPs.

HOW THE CONSERVATIVE PARTY IS GOVERNED

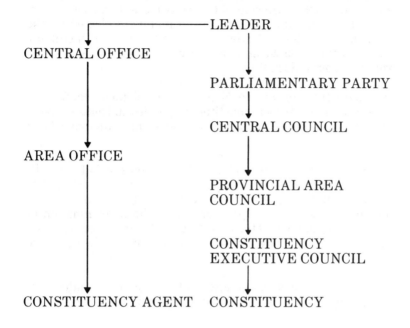

THE LABOUR PARTY

The Labour Party was founded in 1906 and was also an amalgamation of different groups. Its first taste of real power came in 1945, when after the Second World War, Attlee scored a landslide victory at Winston Churchill's expense.

Organisation

The basic unit is again the constituency. Each branch and affiliated organisation (trades unions, Co-operative Party, Young Socialists, socialist societies, etc.) send delegates to the constituency **General Management Committee**, which elects officers and an executive committee and decides local policy.

The constituency will liaise with the officers of the **Regional Councils**, of which there are 11 in England and Wales serviced by a full-time officer employed by party headquarters in Walworth Road, London.

Party decisions and organisation are implemented by the **National Executive Committee**, elected at the **annual conference**, which consists of the party treasurer, 12 members from affiliated trades unions, seven members elected by the constituency Labour Parties, five women's section members, one from the socialist and co-operative societies and another from the Young Socialists.

The main function of the NEC is to implement conference decisions, supervise local constituency parties and enforce party discipline as well as managing finances and employing head office staff.

The leader of the party is elected by the votes of Labour MPs (30%), trades unions (40%) and constituency parties (30%). The annual conference, which is held usually at the end of September, has a much greater say in the determination of party policy than that of the Conservative Party. Delegates from constituencies each have a vote and trades union delegates have a vote in proportion to the strength of their union.

The Shadow Cabinet team is also elected by ballot of Conference, though the actual appointment of specific portfolios is left to the leader.

Parliamentary candidates are selected by branch and trades union delegates to the constituency General Management Committee, not by all members of the party. There are two lists for candidates, one for candidates nominated by trades unions who will, therefore, have union funding for an election, the other for candidates nominated by constituency parties and who are less likely to have sponsorship or funding to finance a general election campaign.

Sitting MPs have to put themselves forward for reselection to the GMC before each general election. Candidates can be deselected if they lose the support of their constituency parties.

THE LABOUR PARTY CHAIN OF COMMAND LOOKS LIKE THIS:—

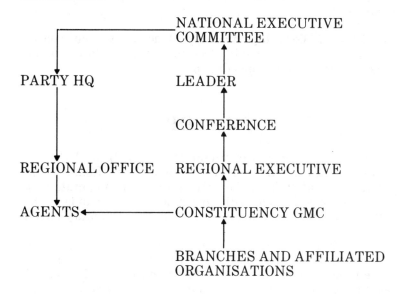

THE LIBERAL PARTY

The Liberal Party evolved from the Whigs who had represented the merchant class against the landed gentry. Their name emerged out of the 1932 Reform Act and although initially used as a term of abuse was later taken up by members to imply commitment to social reform and progressive legislation.

Organisation

Constituencies form the base of the organisation, these in turn being grouped into provincial area organisations. But major policy is decided at party conference, usually held in mid September.

The Liberal Party is very much committed to devolved decision-making and has an anti-centralist approach in terms of hierarchy.

The Leader of the party is selected by a vote of all members of the party by ballot. MPs have the same voting rights as ordinary members.

The **Liberal Assembly**, made up of delegates from constituencies throughout Britain, decides on party policy and can reject leadership recommendations.

THE SDP

Formed by a breakaway group of four Labour MPs and ministers, Roy Jenkins, Shirley Williams, Bill Rodgers and David Owen after 1979, the SDP has sought to operate as a centralist organisation, with power held in the hands of the **Council for Social Democracy** and the Parliamentary Party.

The break with the Labour Party was a combination of personality clashes and ideology, particularly over fears of extreme left-wing infiltration of the Labour Party. The "rebels" feared the Labour Party was moving into dangerous waters especially on defence issues and on Britain's membership of the Common Market.

The 1983 and 1987 general elections were contested by the Liberal and SDP parties under the joint banner of the Alliance, with each party within the Alliance selecting candidates for specific seats.

After their bad result in 1987, pressure mounted for the two parties to merge. The majority of the SDP agreed, but a sizeable rump did not, and pledged to remain a separate party.

David Owen was implacably opposed to merger and immediately resigned as SDP leader on losing the ballot of members. He retains the support of most SDP MPs, who have pledged to oppose the outright merger.

The merging of the SDP and Liberals is currently under discussion and has the approval of both parties. They hope to unite in the summer of 1988 under a joint leader to be elected by all members.

There was a set back to these plans when some senior Liberals announced that they would not join the new party.

PARTY ORGANISATION

Party Agents

Each party has agents who act as secretaries to the constituency parties, and at general elections are responsible for the conduct of campaigns and are legally and financially responsible. These can be either full-time, paid party officials or voluntary helpers. The Conservative Party has the most full-timers with the other parties having only a few.

Party Finance

The main political parties derive their funds from various sources.

The Conservative Party gains its income from voluntary subscriptions, from individuals as well as private companies and businesses. There is no fixed subscription.

The Labour Party gains most of its income from trades union subscriptions. In 1988, individual members were paying £10-£60 a year with reduced rates for students, the elderly and the unemployed.

The Liberal Party gains its income from individual donations and fund-raising schemes. The minimum subscription is £10, with a reduction for the unemployed.

The SDP has no fixed subscription though members and supporters are asked to pay a minimum of £4 a year.

No political party is legally obliged to publish its accounts. But under the Companies Act of 1967, businesses must publish their accounts and record contributions to political party funds, which exceed £200.

PRESSURE GROUPS

In drawing up their manifestos political parties would be doing themselves a disservice if they did not take a very large number of opinions into account. To attract the widest possible support they must settle upon the issues which most concern people and give voice to those feelings when they make their election promises.

That is not to say that minority views are ignored. Strong pressure groups such as the trades unions and those representing industry, agriculture, mining, the elderly and protectors of the Sunday Observance Laws demand to know where a party stands on issues close to their hearts. Some concessions are generally thought to be desirable where they do not conflict with the party's determination to press ahead with radical reform.

CHAPTER 5

ELECTIONS

Describes the Parliamentary electoral system, the work of the Boundary Commissions and lists the legal requirements for candidates and voters.

Britain is divided into 650 **constituencies,** each containing between 60,000 and 70,000 electors. Constituency boundaries are reviewed on a regular basis by the Parliamentary Boundary Commissions to ensure the average number of electors is kept constant and to keep a check on demographic change.

Boundary Commissions

There are four Boundary Commissions, one each for England, Wales, Scotland and Northern Ireland.

Their role is to review the size of constituencies and make reports to the Home Secretary on any changes or redistribution that may be necessary to take into account population changes.

The Home Secretary and the government of the day need not accept the recommendations. In practice, if it means they stand to lose seats by the change, they will not implement them.

The commission is required to review the boundaries at least once a decade.

In 1983, the commission undertook the greatest boundary change since the 1832 Reform Act.

The number of constituencies was increased from 635 to

650, with only 66 constituency boundaries remaining unchanged.

Minor changes to boundaries were made in another 43 constituencies. This meant that 541 constituency boundaries were radically altered.

Voting Rules

The 1969 Representation of the People Act gave the vote to all electors, aged 18 and over and also allowed for the first time a political description of a candidate of up to six words to appear on the ballot paper.

In 1986, the **election deposit** was raised to £500, to be forfeited if a candidate polled less than five percent of the total votes cast in the constituency. The aim of this was to discourage frivolous fringe candidates from standing. Despite this the 1986 Greenwich by-election, won by Rosie Barnes of the SDP, produced a candidate under the party label of "Rainbow Alliance Beer Fags Loony Skittles-Party".

Election Expenditure

Once a candidate is adopted during the General Election campaign, he must declare all his election expenses. Overspending can lead to his disqualification or the disqualification and imprisonment of his agent. In 1980, the agent of Tory MP, Norman St. John Stevas, in Chelmsford, was convicted of such overspending, as was the agent of Labour MP, John Ryman, in Blyth, in the late 1970s.

Current maximum expenses are £3,240, plus a few pence for every entry on the electoral roll.

Qualifications for Voting

Voters must be over 18, be a British, Irish or Commonwealth citizen and be on the electoral register for the area. This operates from February 16 each year, having been compiled under the eye of the electoral registration officer, the previous October. It can now be updated monthly and is the same register as that used at local election times.

Disqualifications from Voting

Peers cannot vote in a Parliamentary Election. Those serving a prison or borstal sentence of one year or more are barred until they have served their sentence. Persons convicted of corrupt or illegal electoral practices are disqualified for five years from their conviction. Persons of unsound mind — defined as those committed to mental institutions under medical orders — are also disqualified from voting.

Voting Procedure

There are three ways of voting, in person at a polling station on polling day, by post if there are medical grounds, or by proxy.

A voter absent for some reason on polling day (e.g. on armed service or abroad in the merchant navy) may nominate someone to attend the polling station to vote on his behalf. From 1986, holidaymakers were allowed a **postal** or **proxy vote**, so were people living abroad providing they have been on the electoral register during the last five years.

Qualifications for Candidacy

Candidates must be over 21, and be a British, Irish or Commonwealth citizen. A parliamentary candidate need not live in the constituency for which he is standing.

Disqualifications from Candidacy

A person cannot be a candidate if he has been sentenced to a term of imprisonment of three months or more during the five years preceding an election, or has been found guilty of corrupt or illegal practices in an election (bribery, cheating, impersonation).

Peers cannot stand for Parliament, nor can senior civil servants, holders of judicial office, regular members of the Armed Forces and members of the police force. Clergy of the Church of England, Church of Scotland, Church in Ireland and the Roman Catholic Church are also disbarred from standing for Parliament.

Bankrupts cannot stand for five years after their discharge. Committed patients in mental institutions are also disqualified from standing.

Any dispute as to qualification is referred to the **Committee of Privileges.**

The Election Procedure

Notice of an election must be given at least 25 days in advance. Nominations close at noon on the 19th day before the day of election (excluding Sundays and Bank Holidays). Notice of withdrawal from the nomination must be given by noon on the 16th day before the day of election, and official notice of the poll must be posted on or before the sixth day before the day of election.

A candidate must have a proposer, seconder and eight assentors, all of whom must live in the constituency and be on the electoral roll. The **Returning Officer**, normally the Chief Executive of the District Council, has the right to refuse a nomination if the nomination papers are not in order.

Until a general election or a by-election is called, candidates are **prospective parliamentary candidates** for their particular parties. Once the election is announced, they are officially adopted by their parties as the candidate. The constituency party is then dissolved until after the election, with the election agent being legally responsible for the party.

From then on the candidate must declare all his election expenses (e.g. cost of printing the election address, the cost of envelopes, the hiring of halls for meetings, payment of speakers). This overall cost must be submitted to the Returning Officer, who must publish the returns and deposit them for inspection by members of the press and public.

Election Agents

During an election, each candidate must appoint an election agent who is legally responsible for all literature published and for ensuring the expenditure limits are not exceeded. The agent is also overall head of constituency party organisation during this period and its business manager.

CHAPTER 6

THE EUROPEAN COMMUNITY

An outline of the role of the major institutions of the EC and elections to the European Parliament.

Renunciation of some national sovereignty is inevitable as nations identify a need for common defence and economic policies.

When NATO was formed much of Britain's defence strategy had to bow to the greater demands of the organisation and with the advent of the Common Market, decisions not always to the liking of the populace were suddenly forced upon what had hitherto been a fiercely independent nation. In a fast changing world sovereign claims were having to be modified in the interests of joint international action.

The Treaty of Rome, signed by Belgium, France, West Germany, Italy, Luxemburg and the Netherlands in 1957, set up the **European Economic Community** (recently renamed the European Community) with the aim of promoting a continuous and balanced economic expansion by establishing a common market and progressively putting the economics of Member States onto a similar footing.

Among the basic objectives of the EC are the founding of an ever closer union among the peoples of Europe, the improvement of their living and working conditions, the progressive abolition of restrictions on trade and the development of the prosperity of overseas countries.

Britain, with the Irish Republic and Denmark, joined the

original Six on January 1, 1973. A national referendum endorsed Britain's membership in 1975. In 1981, Greece joined and in 1986, Portugal and Spain, making a total of 12 countries.

How it all began

Five years before the Treaty of Rome, the Six joined in the European Coal and Steel Community setting up a Common Market for coal and steel and forming the pattern for the community approach to economic integration.

The **European Energy Commission** (EURATUM) was set up in 1957. Since 1959 there has been a Common Market for all nuclear materials, while the Community has now established a control system for nuclear materials to prevent their diversion to purposes other than those declared.

The separate institutions established for each of the three communities were merged in 1967. The major institutions of the EC today are:—

The Council of Ministers

The Commission

The Committee of Permanent Representatives

The European Parliament

The European Court of Justice

The Court of Auditors.

The Council of Ministers

The Council is the pivot of the Community, it consists of the ministers of the 12 Member States and its precise membership depends upon the subject under discussion, (e.g. if the subject is agriculture then the agriculture ministers of the Member States attend).

In the event it is the foreign ministers who attend most regularly. The ministers directly represent member governments, indicating that the EC has not yet become what the founding fathers intended — a supra national body — but remains a community of individual states. The Council meets monthly and the chairmanship rotates on a six-monthly basis between the Member States.

The Council is the decision-making body, deciding policy on the basis of proposals from the Commission. Voting is by "weighted majority" except where a Member State, decides a vital matter of national interest is involved when decisions must be unanimous.

Although not provided for in the Treaty of Rome, it has become established that the Heads of State of the member countries meet at least twice a year to discuss broad policy for the EC and the community's attitude to world affairs.

The Commission

The Commissioners are appointed for four years by agreement among Member States. They are pledged to act independently of their home governments and of national or other interests.

Each is responsible for one or more of the Commission's main fields of activity and are answerable to the European Parliament.

The Commission is the watchdog of the EC treaties and may take action against countries or companies who break the rules by either fining them or taking them to the European Court.

The Commission initiates community action by producing policies, draft budgets and draft legislation. It also administers the Community's rules and policies.

A **committee of permanent representatives**, known as COREPER, is made up of the head of each national delegation to the Community. It meets to prepare the ground for the Council of Ministers' meetings and co-ordinate the work of the council's other subordinate bodies and working groups.

European Parliament

The Parliament is directly elected by proportional representation in all member countries apart from the UK (Northern Ireland excluded) where the system is "first past the post". Elections are held every five years, the last being in 1984 when 434 members — their title being Members of the European Parliament (MEPs) — were elected for a five-year term.

There are now 517 MEPs, broken down into the following ratio:

Britain, France, W. Germany, Italy   :   81 each
Spain   :   60
Portugal, Greece, Netherlands, Belgium   :   24 each
Denmark   :   16
Ireland   :   15
Luxemburg   :   6

In Britain the boundaries of the constituencies are drawn by the Boundary Commission and, roughly, are eight House of Commons constituencies grouped together.

People on the electoral register, including peers and ministers of religion, can vote and peers and ministers of religion and British MPs may stand for election. A deposit of £600 is payable and candidates' expenses are limited (£26,000 each in 1984).

Parliament is consulted on and debates all major policy issues and may question the Council of Ministers and the Commission. It has power to dismiss the Commission on a two thirds majority.

Parliament agrees the budget jointly with the Council of Ministers, but can only win concessions by rejecting the budget in its entirety. It examines all draft legislation and can propose amendments.

The Council of Ministers can ignore Parliament's views, but the Council cannot act until Parliament has expressed an opinion. Hence it can delay and use this to win concessions. It can also initiate proposals to the Council of Ministers.

Parliament can influence the institutions through rigorous questioning of the Council of Ministers and the Commission, at Question Time.

The basis of Parliament's activity is in giving opinions on legislation and policy proposals. Each embodies a resolution which goes to the Council of Ministers and may call for amendment in the Commissioner's draft legislation.

The Court of Justice

The Court interprets and adjudicates on the meaning of the treaties and any measure taken by the Council of Ministers and the Commission under those treaties. It hears appeals and

54

complaints brought by or against the institution, Member States or individuals and gives preliminary rulings on questions referred to it by State courts. As the court of final appeal, decisions are binding on States, institutions and individuals. The Court consists of nine judges, assisted by four advocates general.

Court of Auditors

This court was set up in 1977 and carries out a continuous audit of the handling of community funds by Member States and institutions.

CHAPTER 7

HOME AFFAIRS

An explanation of the role of the Home Office with special reference to the police, prison service and fire service.

F ew government departments have such wide ranging responsibilities as the Home Office, dealing as it does with all domestic matters in England and Wales not specifically assigned to other departments.

The department is headed by the Home Secretary or, to give him his full title, the Secretary of State for the Home Department. He is assisted by two Ministers of State — not of Cabinet rank —and a Parliamentary Under Secretary. An important function is to keep channels of communication open between the Crown and subjects and between the Crown and the Established Church. He is also the government's link between the Channel Islands and the Isle of Man.

The Home Secretary administers a wide variety of statute law which bears strongly on the well-being of the individual. For instance, he deals with matters concerning community relations, immigration and naturalisation, the supervision and deportation of aliens, equal opportunities for women, sex discrimination and obscenity, liquor licensing, gaming and lotteries, theatres and cinemas, music and dancing, shop hours and charitable collections.

But it is in the field of law and order where the Home Secretary's prime responsibilities lie. He is particularly concerned with the administration of justice and the criminal law, sometimes in conjunction with the Lord Chancellor.

Other responsibilities in this area include:—

- Organisation of magistrates courts

- Appointments of Metropolitan and stipendary magistrates

- Treatment of offenders (in prisons but also during probation, parole or after care).

- Advising the Queen on the granting of Royal Pardons or the exercise of mercy.

Parole

In England and Wales prisoners serving sentences of more than 10½ months become eligible for release on parole licence when they have served one third of their sentence or six months, whichever is the longer. In Scotland they qualify after six months. Parole is granted only in exceptional circumstances to those serving for five years or more for violence or drug trafficing. The parole licence lays down conditions for release, including maintaining contact with a supervising officer and remains in force until the date the sentence would have been completed.

The Home Secretary is advised on release of prisoners on licence by the Parole Board, an independent body which includes judges and doctors.

The release of those serving life sentences is at the discretion of the Home Secretary or the Scottish Secretary, subject to the favourable recommendation by the **Parole Board** and often consulting the judiciary though they are not bound to accept these views.

Police Service

The Home Secretary has wide powers over the police service. As well as being in overall charge of the Metropolitan Police as the police authority for Greater London, he also has indirect but effective control of police forces throughout the country.

Training, conditions of service and regulation of all forces is the responsibility of the Home Secretary who must also approve the appointment of Chief Constables and their deputies.

An inspectorate reports on efficiency and organisation and the Home Secretary can amalgamate forces or insist on co-operation between them. A Chief Constable's retirement in the interests of efficiency could also happen on instructions from the Home Office.

The Home Secretary holds the ultimate power of withholding or reducing government grants to all police authorities and has oversight of supporting services such as forensic science.

Police forces are recruited and managed locally with the exception of the Metropolitan force. In England and Wales **police committees** or authorities perform this function but whatever its title, the governing body should comprise two-thirds councillors and one-third magistrates. In Scotland police authorities are the regional and island councils, while the Northern Ireland authority is appointed by the Secretary of State.

Police authorities' responsibilities include the appointment of the **chief constable**, deputy and assistant chief constables, fixing the maximum size of the force and providing buildings and equipment. As indicated, many of these functions are subject to approval by the Home Secretary.

Chief constables are responsible for the operational control of their forces and the appointment, promotion and discipline of their men below the rank of assistant chief constable. They are generally answerable to their police authority on the efficiency of their force and must submit an annual report.

Fire Service and Civil Defence

In the discharge of his duties of ensuring public safety, the Home Secretary has control of the country's fire services in much the same way as he controls the police service.

He exercises this control through the approval of the appointment of chief fire officers, the regulation of training and fire cover and, through an inspectorate, the efficiency of the service. The Civil Defence and emergency service are subject to similar supervision.

Other responsibilities

The list of the Home Secretary's responsibilities is by no means exhausted.Conduct of Parliamentary and local goverment **elections**, scrutiny of some local goverment **bylaws**, regulation of scientific experiments on animals, supervision of controls on explosives, firearms and dangerous drugs, ordering of exhumation and removal of bodies, regulation of cremations and burials, all come within his purview.

Apart from advising the Monarch on the exercise of the **Royal Pardon**, the Home Secretary is responsible for the ceremonial and formal business in connection with the bestowal of honours such as preparing patents of nobility for peers. He also has the duty of presenting petitions and addresses to the Queen and to Parliament.

CHAPTER 8
HEALTH AND WELFARE SERVICES

In July 1988, as we were going to press, Mrs Thatcher decided to split the Department of Health and Social Security into two separate ministries. Description of the administration structure of the National Health Service and an explanation of the welfare benefits available through the DHSS.

Of all government departments the Department of Health and Social Security is the one which most closely touches the individual, responsible as it is for the welfare and health services which are designed to give aid and support when needed to the individual throughout his life.

It is responsible for the administration (in England) of the National Health Service, the social services provided by local authorities for the elderly, the handicapped, socially deprived and also aspects of public health, including hygiene.

Payment of benefit under National Insurance and non-contributory benefits, including **child benefit** (previously called family allowance), as well as the collection of contributions to the **National Insurance**, are also its responsibility. The provision of reception centres for vagrants and others without homes, pensions and welfare services for war pensioners and assessing the means of applicants for legal aid, also come under the DHSS umbrella.

The department is headed by a Secretary of State (a Cabinet post) assisted by two Ministers of State (one for Health and one for Social Services) and three Parliamentary Under Secretaries.

NATIONAL HEALTH SERVICE

The National Health Service, set up in 1948 and subject to several re-organisations since, is based on the principle that medical care and advice should be readily available to everyone at little or no cost.

The service is financed largely from general taxation, plus revenue from charges for such items as prescriptions, dental and opthalmic services, and in small part from the national insurance contributions.

The Health Ministers — the Secretary of State for Social Services in England and the Secretaries of State for Scotland, Wales and Northern Ireland — are responsible for all aspects of the health service in their respective areas.

They are included on a **Supervisory Board** which advises on strategy, while the NHS **Management Board** has the task of giving leadership to the service, controlling and monitoring performance and instilling consistency and drive.

Regional Health Authorities

England is divided into 14 **Regional Authorities** (RHAs) each covering several counties or major towns or cities, whose chairmen and members are appointed by the Secretary of State. These authorities are responsible for strategic, long term planning, including major building programmes and for monitoring the performance of District Health Authorities (DHAs).

Each region receives a yearly allocation of funds from the Government and has the duty of sharing this cash between the district authorities and regional services, monitoring how the cash is spent and ensuring the DHAs keep within their budgets.

District Health Authorities

There are 192 **District Health Authorities** within the regions who are responsible for running the local hospitals and community services and keeping within the cash limits set down by the RHAs.

The DHAs have a chairman appointed by the Secretary of State and usually 16 members appointed by the region which include nominees of local authorities within the district, a hospital consultant, a general medical practitioner, and a nurse, midwife or health visitor. The balance comes from outside the health movement, including a trade union representative.

Districts are further divided into units of management which can be either a large hospital, a group of hospitals, a geographical area or type of service (e.g. mentally handicapped or community service).

In 1984, after an inquiry into management of the hospital service, headed by Sir Roy Griffiths, managing director of Sainsburys, the government accepted the case for general managers who would take direct and personal responsibility for the services they run.

General managers have now been appointed at regional, district and unit level. Although they replace the teams which existed until the mid 1980's most still operate by drawing on the skills and experience of a management group.

Community Health Councils

Each District Health Authority has a matching Community Health Council which represents the interests of the users of the Health Service. Its members are drawn from local authorities and voluntary organisations and others with an interest in health.

The council's role is to comment on services provided and on the plans of the District Health Authority. An annual report is produced and this provides useful material for discussion with the DHA. Meetings of the CHC are open to press and public.

Family Practitioner Committees

The administrative arrangements for the work of general practitioners, dentists, pharmacists, and opticians are the duties of Family Practitioner Committees which are independent health authorities.

There are 98 of them usually matching county boundaries, except in the conurbations. The chairman and members are appointed by the Secretary of State, and include lay people as well as members from the professions. The committees adjudicate on complaints made against practitioners.

Wales, Scotland and Northern Ireland

There are no regional authorities in Wales. The nine District Health Authorities, each with a Family Practitioner Committee covering its area, are responsible direct to the Secretary of State for Wales.

In Scotland there are 15 Health Boards combining the functions of the English RHAs and DHAs and with a **Primary Care Division** which arranges contracts with general practitioners, dentists, pharmacists and opticians. There are also **Local Health Councils** which equate to the Community Health Councils in England and Wales.

As well as their duties as health authorities, the four **Health and Social Services Boards** in Northern Ireland administer the social services provided by English local authorities.

Ambulance Service

Although the ambulance service was transferred from the county councils to health authorities, it is still largely based on the old areas and in many cases retains the old name (e.g. London, Kent, East Sussex Ambulance Service). But it is managed by one District Health Authority on behalf of the others within the geographical area.

Health Service Commissioner

Provision is made for Health Service Commissioners (Ombudsmen) for England, Wales and Scotland but all three offices are held by the Parliamentary Commissioner for Administration.

His health service jurisdiction covers the failure of a health authority to carry out its statutory duty, complaints of maladministration and injustice or hardship caused by a failure in a service.

The complaint must first be sent to the health authority concerned which must be given sufficient time to investigate and reply.

Matters of clinical judgement are outside his jurisdiction.

He publishes at regular intervals full reports of his investigations, but omits names of individuals or institutions. The report is sent to the authority complained about and to the administrative tier above. The complainant may receive an explanation or apology. The Commissioner also reports annually to the Health Ministers who lay an official document before Parliament.

In Northern Ireland the Commissioner for Complaints investigates Health Service complaints.

Problems facing the Health Service

The Health Service is currently the centre of controversy and political debate. It has undergone a number of organisational changes (1974, 1982 and 1984) and further radical changes are being debated. The major problems may be summarised as follows:

STRUCTURAL — The boundaries of the health districts bear no relation to local authority boundaries, making liaison with the social service authorities difficult. The District Health Authorities are required by law to set up **joint consultative committees** with the local authority social service authorities in order to plan and provide joint services.

Some people argue that the structure is too hospital orientated at the expense of community services. Others claim that it is over bureaucratic.

PRIVATE MEDICINE — Ever since the establishment of the NHS, doctors have been permitted to engage in private practice. This can take place in private hospitals or in private beds within the NHS. Out of the half a million beds within the NHS, 3,000 are occupied by private patients. The private sector only caters for about 10% of patients but some observers fear that an increase in private medicine may lead to a two-tier service. Others argue that private medicine benefits the NHS by relieving pressure on it and gives patients freedom of choice as well as promoting competition.

FINANCE — The health service cost about £21,314m in 1987-88, some 5.4% of the gross domestic product. About 86% is paid for by general taxes, the rest comes from charges and part of the National Insurance contributions. The major political debate is on whether sufficient is spent on health. The Government points out that it is spending more on health, taking into account inflation, than any other government in history. The critics argue that though this may be true, it is not enough. They point out that the number of elderly in the community is increasing, putting additional strain on the NHS and medical inflation is higher than general inflation. This requires an increase of two percent above the rate of inflation just to keep pace.

SOCIAL SECURITY

A comprehensive social security system was set up under a series of Acts in the 1940s and became operative in 1948.

It has been amended by a number of Acts since then and is currently undergoing a major reform. It still remains a comprehensive system designed to secure a basic standard of living for people in financial need by providing income support during periods of inability to earn due to illness, disablement or unemployment and to help those who are retired, widowed or bringing up children.

Social Security benefits fall into two broad categories — contributory or non-contributory. The former are paid from the National Insurance Fund to which employed people and their employers, self-employed people and the government contribute. Non-contributory benefits are financed from general taxation. Entitlement depends solely on meeting the qualifying conditions.

Contributory Benefits

These include national insurance, retirement and widows

pensions, sickness and invalidity benefits, unemployment and maternity pay (paid directly by the woman's employer) or maternity allowance (a flat rate paid by the DHSS to those who do not qualify for maternity pay).

Non-Contributory Benefits

These include **child benefit** (a tax free benefit usually paid to the mother for all children), **attendance allowance, invalid care allowance, mobility allowance, war pensions.** Also included are **income support** (which replaced supplementary benefit in April 1988) paid to those not in work who prove they have insufficient to live on; **family credit** (replaced family income supplement) paid to working families, with children, earning below the poverty line; **housing benefit** (replaced the housing benefit scheme) and offers help with rent and rates.

Loans or grants to those who have special or emergency needs and are without sufficient means are paid from the **Social Fund**, introduced in 1987. It replaced the death grant and maternity grant and now covers budgeting and crisis loans to help the poor meet important intermittent expenses.

Appeals

All applicants for Social Security benefits have the right of appeal if rejected or the amount offered is thought insufficient. The appeal is against the ruling of an adjudicating officer or an adjudicating medical officer.

The appeal goes to either a **Social Security Appeal Tribunal** (SSAT) or a **Medical Appeal Tribunal** (MAT).

The former is composed of a chairman (usually a lawyer) and two others and the chairman is accompanied by two consultant doctors.

Both tribunals are independent of the DHSS and Department of Employment and appeals against their decisions — on points of law only — are to a **Social Security Commissioner** who is an independent lawyer.

CHAPTER 9

EMPLOYMENT

*The roles of the Department of Trade and Industry, the
Department of Employment and the Manpower Services
Commission (Training Commission) in improving
employment prospects and encouraging training.*

Throughout this century governments have become more and more involved in controlling the economy and attempting to stimulate employment and industry. There is debate between the political parties as to how far this intervention should go.

Three government departments are involved in framing government economic, employment and industrial policy. They are the Treasury, the Department of Employment and the Department of Trade and Industry.

The Treasury is responsible for overall economic and fiscal policy — particularly in determining public expenditure levels and taxation policy. The **Department of Employment** is concerned with manpower policy and industrial relations, including safety at work. The **Department of Trade and Industry** is responsible for regional industrial policy, company law, take-overs and mergers, and international trade.

In early 1988 the Department of Trade and Industry published a White Paper entitled: "The Department of Trade and Industry — The Department for Enterprise". This policy document signalled a fundamental shift in policy for the department. Regional aid was no longer to be automatic but was to become selective; greater support would be given to small companies; the department wanted to launch a major new initiative to encourage marketing, design and management skills in small

69

and medium sized companies; links between industry and education were to be strengthened and the DTI was to make more money available to education to encourage the use of information technology.

In order to help small companies the Department of Trade and Industry planned to expand its regional offices and set up satellite offices in Chambers of Commerce to give consultancy advice.

Unemployment is a major problem in the United Kingdom as it is in many countries of the world. By 1980 the number of people out of work had risen to 8.3 percent of the population and this figure rose to a peak of around 12 per cent in 1986.

The situation didn't improve until the latter half of 1987 but by the arrival of the new year unemployment had fallen to below the three million mark and the prediction was that this trend would continue during 1988.

Unemployment affected all parts of the United Kingdom but certain areas were hit more severely than others.

Two strategies to try to alleviate unemployment problems were put forward, one aiming to attract industry to areas of high unemployment, the other helping the unemployed to find jobs.

Attracting Industry to Areas of Unemployment

Inducements to industry to set up in areas of high unemployment are provided by central government (Department of Trade and Industry), local government and the EEC. In Wales the Welsh Office and the Welsh Development Agency encourage new industrial development.

Central Government may designate **assisted areas (Development Areas** and **Intermediate Areas)** and provide incentives for companies to move there and set up business. In January 1988 the Government announced changes in the grants. **Regional Selective Grants** will only be paid if the project would not proceed without financial assistance. In addition, training grants may be available to companies in these areas. Prior to this change in policy, grants were automatically available to companies in assisted areas.

The Government may also set up **Enterprise Zones** (Local Government, Planning and Land Act 1980). These zones may either cover a whole town or just part of a town. Currently there are around 25 enterprise zones. Within such zones planning procedures are simplified, industry and commerce are exempt from rates and are given certain tax benefits.

The Department of Trade and Industry has set up 16 task forces, comprising civil servants from a number of government departments, to try to stimulate employment in the inner cities.

Finally, government may set up **Urban Development Corporations**. They will buy the land at market value and redevelop the area to attract industry and commerce. Examples of such corporations are London Docklands and Merseyside.

Local authorities have become far more active in trying to attract industry and employment to their areas in recent years. They may set up industrial development corporations of their own, acquire land to sell or rent to companies, provide new industrial sites and build advanced factory sites (often in co-operation with private developers).

Local authorities can also improve existing industrial sites and enhance the general environment as an incentive to companies to move to their area. Partnership schemes between central and local government may be set up under the Urban Programme to revitalise the run down inner cities.

The European Community makes money available to central government, local government and even individual companies to encourage industrial development in areas of high unemployment. The money will come in the form of grants or loans.

It is usually only forthcoming for areas designated as having high unemployment and normally any money from the EC has to be matched with money from the national government.

Grants are available from the **European Coal and Steel Community** for areas which have suffered redundancies in these industries, and from the **European Regional** and **Social Funds**.

Helping the Unemployed Find Jobs

There are now many and varied schemes for helping the unemployed find jobs, bridging the skills gap, encouraging employers to take on the unemployed or helping people to start up their own business.

Some of the schemes are the responsibility of the **Manpower Services Commission**, a Quango* set up by the Training and Employment Act 1973. Under the Act responsibility for training and employment was transferred from a government department to a body which represents employees, local government and education.

The MSC currently consists of a full-time chairman, appointed by the Secretary of State for Employment and accountable to him, three industrialists, three unionists, two representatives of local government and one representative of education.

The MSC was originally responsible for planning, developing and operating the public employment and training services. But in 1987 some of its employment responsibilities were moved back under the umbrella of the Department of Employment leaving the MSC to concentrate more on training services. The MSC is to be renamed the **Training Commission**.

Training Services

The major function of the MSC is to ensure that the unemployed and school leavers have the skills and qualifications to get a job. In addition to the schemes mentioned below, the MSC funds 25 per cent of non-advanced further education which gives the commission a major say over a large number of courses provided in further education colleges.

> **Youth Training Scheme:** This scheme is for 16/17-year-old school leavers. It provides for one or two year training schemes, including work experience and 20 weeks off-the-job training. Trainees receive an allowance, currently

---

Footnote: **QUANGO** stands for quasi autonomous non-governmental organisation. There are many such creatures, the members of which are appointed by the government usually from representatives of employers, trade unions and local government. The organisations are funded by the government and are answerable to the government but the staff are strictly not civil servants and they enjoy some autonomy.

£27.30 per week for the first year and £35 for the second year. The schemes take place in industry, commerce and the public sector.

Job Training Scheme: This scheme is for anyone over 18 who has been out of education for at least two years and is unemployed. The programme involves work experience and off-the-job training and is provided in industry and commerce, in colleges and MSC skill centres. Industry and commerce make a financial contribution but most of the cost is born by the MSC. The trainees receive an allowance while on the scheme. In late 1987 the Government announced that this scheme will be changed and it may be combined with the Community Programme.

In February 1988 the Government issued a White Paper, "Training for Employment", which outlines the new policy. The new scheme, which will start in September 1988, will guarantee up to a year's training for young adults who have been unemployed for more than six months. For those between 25 and 50 the Government hopes to introduce a similar guarantee after they have been unemployed for two years.

Participation in the scheme will be voluntary, trainees will receive a payment slightly in excess of their current benefit payments together with additional payments to cover transport and child care costs. The participants will receive counselling and training in basic skills of literacy and numeracy as well as higher technical skills. The MSC will provide some money to cover the training costs but employers will have to make a contribution.

Job Training Grants: The MSC will provide grants to employers and advice on how to train or retrain their staff.

In addition to the three main schemes mentioned above the MSC also runs numerous smaller schemes for small groups of workers.

Employment Services

In an attempt to provide a more comprehensive service to unemployed job seekers, the Department of Employment decided that some reorganisation was necessary in 1987.

Job centres which advise the unemployed and the employed of job vacancies — as well as employers of the manpower situation in any area — were taken away from the MSC. By way of explanation, the Government said it wanted to provide a closer working relationship between the job centres and the Unemployment Benefit Service.

At the same time the department took over from the MSC responsibility for the following services:—

Restart Programme: A scheme designed for those who have been unemployed for a year. They are offered a suitable job, temporary employment on a Community Programme, a place in a Job Club, the chance to become self-employed, a training scheme, a Jobstart Allowance, or a Restart Course. The latter lasts from one to two weeks and will help the unemployed determine the type of job most suitable to his qualifications.

Jobstart Allowance: Currently £20 is paid for six months to those who have been out of work for a year or more and who take a job paying less than £80 per week. The aim is to get them back into the work environment.

Community Programme: For those who have been unemployed for either six months or a year, depending on age. The scheme lasts a year and involves projects in the community — e.g. clearing derelict land. The unemployed are paid the rate for the job.

New Workers' Scheme: This is for the young unemployed. An employer who takes on a young unemployed person (under 21) and pays below a set wage (£55 and £65 per week depending on age) receives £15 per week for a year towards the employee's wages.

Job Clubs: These are run by Job Centres for the long term unemployed. The clubs are based on self-help and provide the environment, facilities and support to help the unemployed seek work.

Enterprise Allowance Scheme: Under this scheme an unemployed person is given a weekly allowance if he sets himself up in business. He has to be able to raise £1,000 himself and must have been unemployed for eight weeks. The allowance is £40 per week.

Professional and Executive List: A special service to place professional, administerial and managerial staff who are seeking work.

In addition, the department took over sheltered employment and services for the disabled.

CHAPTER 10

INDUSTRY

Explanation of the Department of Employment's responsibility for industrial relations and safety at work; nationalised industries and the move towards privatisation.

The Secretary of State for Employment has overall responsibility for industrial relations and industrial law, including any legislation connected with trade unions.

Since 1974, when The **Advisory Conciliation and Arbitration Service** (ACAS) was set up to provide conciliation to private and public companies, he has not been directly involved in settling industrial disputes. If all official channels have been exhausted, and if both sides agree, an arbitrator or a board of arbitrators will be appointed to try to bring the parties together and reach agreement.

ACAS cannot impose a settlement and its existence does not prevent the Secretary of State for Employment trying to solve industrial disputes either personally or by setting up a Court of Inquiry or a Commission of Investigation. In practice, however, governments have kept out of industrial disputes and left their solution to ACAS and the parties involved.

The Department of Employment issues work permits to non-EC nationals, permitting them to work in this country. It also runs the quota scheme for the disabled, whereby all employers employing more than 20 should, if possible, employ three percent who are registered disabled.

SAFETY AT WORK

The State's concern for safety at work has increased over the years. Legislation exists for various industries but since the Safety at Work Act 1974 all industries, not covered by specific legislation, are subject to an all-embracing Act.

The Safety at Work Act puts a duty on both the employer and the employee. The employer is under a duty to provide a safe work environment and provide and maintain safe equipment. The employee must take reasonable care not to put himself or others at risk and must not interfere with safety guards.

The Act set up two corporate bodies — the Health and Safety Commission and the Health and Safety Executive.

Health and Safety Commission

The Health and Safety Commission comprises representatives of employers, trade unions and local authorities, appointed by the Secretary of State for Employment. Its role is to decide on policy and to propose new regulations, which are then enacted by the minister who has overall responsibility for the industry.

Health and Safety Executive

The Health and Safety Executive is the operational arm of the Commission and controls the enforcement agencies like the Factory Inspectorate, Mines Inspectorate, and the Nuclear Installations Inspectorate.

The inspectors visit places of work and inspect them for safety and will also investigate after a serious accident has occurred. They have wide powers and may serve an **improvement notice** which instructs the employer to make certain improvements before a set date. They may also serve a **prohibition notice** which instructs the employer to cease using certain equipment until changes are made, or the Executive can prosecute.

Local authority **environmental health officers** are responsible for enforcing the legislation in non-industrial premises, (e.g. service industries, places of entertainment, offices, etc.)

NATIONALISED INDUSTRIES

Nationalisation has been a key issue at British general elections since the second world war. Since 1979, however, debate has intensified and nationalisation versus privatisation has rarely been out of the political arena.

The bulk of nationalisation was undertaken by the Labour Government of Attlee between 1945-50. This sprang from the desire to control the economy by keeping a firm grip on the basic industries of coal, steel, energy and transport. At one time the Conservative party supported the mixed economy and, in fact, the Heath Government did nationalise two ailing companies. But the policy changed with the 1979 General Election.

The Thatcher Government embarked on a major privatisation programme, selling off most of the nationalised industries to private shareholders. The Government's belief was that once under the private sector these industries would become more responsive to consumer demand, more efficient and would be freed from political control.

Small investors were encouraged to invest in the privatisation schemes and this has become a major plank in Mrs. Thatcher's wish for a shareholding democracy. As a result the British National Oil Corporation, Cable and Wireless, British Freight Corporation, British Airways, British Telecom, British Gas, the National Bus Company, Sealink, and many ports have been privatised.

The Labour party's rigid stance on nationalisation started to modify after a third successive general election defeat. In 1987 the party's attitude to full blown nationalisation underwent re-examination and there was talk of "social ownership" which has been seen by many as a half-way house between re-nationalisation and privatisation.

Organisation of Nationalised Industries

The so-called nationalised industries are, in fact, organised as **public corporations** and do not operate as government departments. The industries are vested in a public corporation, created by statute. There are no shareholders.

The corporation is headed by a board which is responsible for the industry. The board is appointed by the Government and ministers can intervene only so far as statutes permit. The employees are not civil servants and the companies operate like any other company. The board can hire and fire and can be sued.

This method of organisation was adopted to keep these organisations at arm's length from parliamentary and ministerial intervention. Yet despite these intentions, it is clear that parliament and ministers do, in practice, intervene.

CONTROL OF THE NATIONALISED INDUSTRIES

There are three major forms of control over the nationalised industries — parliamentary, ministerial and consumer.

Parliamentary Control

Parliament tends to devote little time to debates on the nationalised industries but MPs do have opportunites to keep an eye on them in two main ways.

Firstly, MPs may ask questions of the sponsoring minister at question time. The sponsoring minister is the minister whose department has ultimate responsibility for the industry. For example, the sponsoring minister for British Steel is the Secretary of State for Trade and Industry and for British Coal, the Secretary of State for Energy.

Ministers are much more willing these days to answer detailed questions about the running of the industries but, as witnessed during the coal strike, they can claim the detailed responsibility lies with the board and not the minister.

Secondly, MPs can use the select committees to question ministers, chairmen and board members, trade unionists and members of the public on any aspect of the nationalised industries.

Ministerial Control

Despite the desire to reduce ministerial intervention in the nationalised industries it is clear that governments and ministers have intervened and made vital decisions affecting many aspects of industrial management. In fact, the Treasury has often exercised more control than the sponsoring department.

Ministers appoint the members of the boards, including the chairmen, and this gives them a great deal of influence over the policy and actions of the corporations. An illustration of this was the choice of Ian McGregor as chairman of the British Coal Board, prior to the miners' strike, in 1984.

Ministers direct the boards on matters considered to be in the national interest, including pricing policy and the provision of loss-making services as a social service.

The investment programmes and the borrowing of money has to be approved by the sponsoring minister. In recent years the nationalised industries have been set targets to achieve and these have had major implications on pricing and staffing levels.

There are two main reasons why ministers intervene. Firstly, to control the economy. The nationalised industries spend a great deal of money on capital equipment and employ vast work forces. As a result, if a government wishes to deflate or reflate the economy one way to do so is to instruct the nationalised industries to spend more or less money on capital equipment. Secondly, the nationalised industries are often monopolies and ministers intervene to ensure that they do not exploit their position.

The Consumer

The consumers have a small voice through the **Consumer and Consultative Councils**. For example, there are Regional Transport Consultative Committees for the railways, Consultative Councils for Electricity and the Post Office Advisory Committees.

The members of these councils are appointed by the sponsoring minister. They will include local authority representatives. The councils look into complaints, consider the level of service

81

provided, the policy of the board and the pricing levels. They report annually to the sponsoring minister.

These consultative councils and committees are a useful contact for the local press when a local consumer angle is required for a story on a nationalised industry.

BRITISH TELECOM

When British Telecom was privatised in 1984 the **Office of Telecommunications (OFTEL)** was set up as an independent regulatory body. OFTEL is a government department, under the Department of Trade and Industry, headed by a director general. Its role is to protect the consumers' interests and is concerned with pricing policy, competition and the quality of service. OFTEL advises the Secretary of State on all matters to do with telecommunications.

Telecommunications is now open to competition which has to be approved by the Secretary of State for Trade and Industry and the Director General of Telecommunications. They issue licences to companies who wish to provide a service.

British Telecom has issued a Code of Practice for consumers. In addition, there are the **National Advisory Committees for Telecommunications** for England, Wales, Scotland and Northern Ireland. Throughout the country there are local **Telecommunications Advisory Committees** to represent the views of the customers and to act as a pressure group on British Telecom.

BRITISH GAS

In 1986 British Gas was privatised and the **Office of Gas Supply (OFGAS)** was set up as an independent regulatory body. Its status is similar to OFTEL but is under the Secretary of State for Energy. Like its counterpart for telecommunication, OFGAS is headed by a Director General.

The major role of OFGAS is to monitor the activities of British Gas, enforce the maximum average price that British Gas can charge and to grant licences to other companies to supply gas through British Gas pipelines. It has a limited role in investigating complaints in that it can only investigate those complaints which relate to its enforcement powers. The major body to represent the consumer is the Gas Consumers' Council.

The **Gas Consumers' Council** was set up in 1986 and replaced 13 autonomous councils. The Council covers England, Wales and Scotland. Its members are appointed by the Department of Trade and Industry and represent the big consumer, the private customer and the regions. Twelve regional offices are situated throughout the country and local volunteers are available to discuss problems with consumers.

The Gas Consumers' Council represents the views of the consumer to the government, British Gas and, unlike the old councils, to any other gas-related company. It has the power to handle complaints from consumers on any matter concerning gas, whether it relates to supply or appliances. The Council produces literature and information, including a card with useful contacts entitled "How we can help journalists".

CHAPTER 11
DEPARTMENT OF THE ENVIRONMENT

An explanation of the role of the Department of the Environment and the measures which can be adopted by central and local government to protect and improve the environment.

The Department of the Environment is responsible for a whole range of functions which affect people's living environment. These include land use planning and development control, inner cities (with the Department of Trade and Industry), housing and general oversight of the construction industry, countryside affairs, sport and recreation, control of pollution of water and sewerage, conservation, and the protection of ancient monuments and historic buildings.

The DOE also looks after the structure and funding of local government as a whole, and plays a major part in regional development. The Welsh Office and the Scottish Development Department have broadly similar responsibilities.

The head of the department is the Secretary of State for the Environment. He is assisted by a team of seven ministers, consisting of a Minister for Housing and Planning, a Minister for Local Government, a Minister of the Environment, and four Parliamentary Under Secretaries of State, one of whom is usually given special responsibility for sport and recreation.

These ministers, together with senior permanent officials, work as a team in major policy decisions, although each minister also takes responsibility under the Secretary of State for specific areas of work.

Although many of the department's staff work in Central

London the DOE has an important presence in the regions. The department's main regional organisation is run jointly with the Department of Transport (until 1976 transport was part of the DOE).

Regional office work includes housing and land use planning, and also broader scale planning for the region as a whole, together with many local transport matters.

Housing

The active role in providing public housing for rent belongs mainly to the local authorities, but the DOE is responsible for the overall framework of national policy and for seeing that local authorities keep within national public expenditure limits.

The DOE supervises the general progress of their housing programmes and activities, including the controversial requirement for council houses to be sold to the tenants. The Government's policy is to encourage home ownership and in line with this, the emphasis of public sector housing has shifted from new building to modernisation of existing buildings.

In the private sector, the DOE is involved in policies on assistance to house purchasers. It maintains continuing discussions with the Building Societies Association on such matters as the amount of mortgage money available for home purchases. This is a vital factor in dictating the number of new homes put on the market by private builders.

The Department is responsible for seeing that fair rents are charged by private landlords and this is operated by **Rent Officers** who, for convenience, in most areas are based at local council offices.

It is also a DOE responsibility to co-ordinate and, in some instances, carry out research into social and technical aspects of housing.

Local Government

Local authorities are independent, democratically elected bodies, created by statute, to whom various Acts of Parliament give responsibilities and powers in local matters. The Department of the Environment is only one of the central government departments involved in providing services in partnership with

86

local authorities, but it is responsible for the structure and overall system of local government, particularly finance.

The Secretary of State has the power to dictate how much can be spent by fixing a maximum level of rates a council can charge, known as **rate capping**. Another powerful curb on local spending powers is the power to withhold selectively the amount of grant given to councils. A limit is set on spending and any council which spends beyond that level can be "fined" by having its grant correspondingly reduced.

Central Government funds are provided in the form of **general and specific grants** and the Secretary of State also controls the amount of money borrowed by local authorities to meet their capital expenditure requirements. In addition, the Secretary of State has a direct interest in the administration by local authorities of a number of specific functions, such as housing, planning and environmental protection.

Planning

Planning involves issues which are varied, complex and very often controversial. Development is often irreversible and so has a bearing on the life of a community for years to come. This makes it necessary for all the implications to be considered carefully before proposals are given the go-ahead — and all the more important for local newspapers to understand and monitor the system on behalf of their readers.

In general, all development requires planning permission, usually decided by local councils. Guidance is given by central government, usually in the form of discussion with planning authorities in a region.

The Secretary of State also approves the **development plans** which local councils draw up — principally the **structure plans** by county councils, **unitary** plans in London and the metropolitan districts and **regional reports** in Scotland. He can also "call in" applications, to be decided by him and not the local councils. Usually these are major developments such as proposed new airports.

It is rare for a Secretary of State to decide upon a major application which has been called in, without holding a full public inquiry. These can often last for months — such as the inquiry into the siting of a new London airport.

Applicants for planning permission also have a right of appeal to the Secretary of State when a local council refuses permission or imposes conditions. Most appeals are dealt with by inspectors (known as reporters in Scotland). Small matters may be decided by written submissions, but major matters are aired at public local inquiries where local people and organisations can make known their views in support of either the appellant or the local councils. In major inquiries inspectors recommend the Secretary of State to refuse, amend or allow the appeal and it is not unknown for a Secretary of State to refuse to follow his inspectors' advice.

Inner Cities

An important present day problem is the decline of the inner city areas, many of which suffer from economic stagnation and physical decay, resulting in bad social conditions. Over the years many industries and businesses have left the inner cities, and as conditions have worsened, private investors became unwilling to risk their money in new ventures there.

In some places the inner city has become a trap for people who are unable to move out namely, the old, the disabled, the unemployed and the unskilled, who are left with poor opportunities in a decaying environment. It is the DOE's responsibility to develop and put into action policies such as the **Urban Programme** to provide "pump-priming" grants to help solve these problems, working jointly with other government departments, local authorities, and voluntary and commercial interests.

Care of Ancient Buildings

There is a wealth of buildings of historic or architectural importance in Britain, and the widespread concern for caring for them is reflected in the existence of many voluntary historical and amenity societies. This concern has resulted in legal protection, the principal one being the **listing** of buildings as being of historic or architectural importance by the Secretary of State.

There are three grades, with Grade 1 being the most exceptional buildings. The purpose is to ensure that they are not demolished or altered without consent of the department. In the rare cases where a building is allowed to be demolished, a photographic record is kept. Any alterations and additions have to be in keeping with the character of the building.

The Secretary of State has the power to "list" a building at any time. The watchdogs are usually local amenity groups and local councils and many a good story has resulted from local worthies thwarting a developer's bulldozer. Usually, the local council serves a **building preservation order** which protects a threatened building for six months to allow consideration of its listing. There are various grant schemes to help owners keep their historic buildings in good repair.

Conservation Areas

It is not buildings alone which are important. Some streets and village centres are important as entities, and local authorities can declare them to be **conservation areas**. These are subject to more stringent planning controls — in broad terms, it is like extending the listing over the whole area. It is the local councils who have the task of declaring conservation areas along guidelines set by the department and then, along with residents and local amenity groups, of setting up schemes to preserve and enhance them.

Historic town centres are also being preserved under **town schemes** in England and Wales. The Secretary of State and the local councils make annual grants available to help keep the buildings in good repair.

The Secretary of State is responsible for maintaining the Royal parks and properties which are open to the public, but in England, it is the **Historic Buildings and Monuments Commission** (known as English Heritage) which protects the country's architectural and archeological treasures. On behalf of the DOE, the commission manages some 400 ancient monuments, and gives grants for ancient monuments and historic buildings in conservation areas. In Scotland, a similar task is undertaken by the **Historic Buildings and Monuments Directorate** of the Scottish Development Department, and in Wales by **Cadw — Welsh Historic Monuments**.

Voluntary Bodies

Much of the work in this field is carried out with the co-operation and support of a number of voluntary and charitable bodies, of which the **National Trust** is perhaps the best known. It is an independent charity with extensive ownership of important buildings and landscape areas throughout the country. Others include the **Civic Trust**, the Society for the Preservation of

Ancient Buildings, the Ancient Monuments Society, the Georgian Group, the Victorian Society, the Council for British Archaeology and the Archaeological Heritage Society of Scotland.

The DOE also encourages high standards in new building and makes annual awards for good housing design in collaboration with the Royal Institute of British Architects and the National Housebuilding Council. Scotland and Wales have similar schemes of their own.

The **Countryside Commission** for England and Wales (and a similar Commission for Scotland) designates national parks and **areas of outstanding natural beauty** which are subject to special planning controls. These have to be confirmed by the appropriate minister. Although the land in such areas remains mostly privately owned, grants are paid to encourage public access through providing car parks and camping grounds, and for tree planting and removing eyesores. In Scotland such areas are called **national scenic areas**.

The Department also sponsors several statutory and chartered agencies which are concerned with recreation and with the countryside, including:

The Development Commission (the development of the rural economy)

The Nature Conservancy Council (nature reserves)

The Sports Council (developing and improving the knowledge and practice of sport and physical recreation).

Pollution

The Government is principally concerned with framing overall policy and giving local authorities the necessary powers to exercise control. There are a number of government departments involved — for example the Department of Transport deals with aircraft noise and marine pollution.

But the main department is the DOE which provides advice generally to local authorities and also co-ordinates all government activities in this field. There are similar arrangements for Wales and Scotland, with the Control of Pollution Act 1974 applying to the whole country. This Act contains most of the powers and duties for local councils and water authorities and controls disposal of wastes, air and water pollution and noise.

Advice is given over the disposal of hazardous wastes — such as asbestos and heavy metals — by **Her Majesty's Inspectorate of Pollution**, which was set up in 1987.It brought together responsibilities for industrial pollution control, and disposal of hazardous wastes which beforehand were split between various government departments. The department, through NIREX —the Nuclear Industry Radioactive Waste Executive — is also investigating sites on land for the disposal of low and intermediate grades of radioactive waste.

Safety of commercial nuclear installations is handled by a specialist section of the Health and Safety Executive, while the primary authority on radiological protection is the National Radiological Protection Board, based at Harwell in Oxfordshire. It checks levels of radioactivity and became better known to the public through its monitoring in the wake of the Chernobyl accident.

The Property Services Agency

The Property Services Agency was created in 1972 as part of the department, and it provides, equips and maintains a wide range of buildings and installations both at home and overseas for government departments, the armed services and many public bodies such as the Post Office and the Manpower Services Commission.

PSA's building programme covers almost every type of construction. For the services, it provides an immense range of facilities from dockyards and airfields to houses, from power stations and water-treatment plants to churches, schools and hospitals. Its civil operations embrace not only office accommodation but also post offices, law courts, prisons, museums and galleries. Many of its projects are highly specialised, particularly those for government research and development establishments.

CHAPTER 12

TRANSPORT

The role of the Department of Transport and its relationship with local government. Planning and maintenance of highways, private transport and road safety.

The Department of Transport is responsible for promoting a safe, efficient and environmentally acceptable transport system for industry and commerce and the general public. This requires a partnership with local authorities and transport operators, and with management and trade unions in both public and private sectors.

The department, while it has some direct involvement, provides the legislation and guidance within which the other sectors operate. For example, local authorities have powers to control traffic but have to follow the department's criteria for introducing such measures as speed limits, weight and height restrictions and pedestrian crossings. Vehicle manufacturers have to follow regulations covering design and materials, the hours of bus and lorry drivers are controlled, and the private motorist has to pass a driving test, obey various traffic laws and not park illegally.

The department also allocates funds to county councils and metropolitan districts in England towards their expenditure on roads and transport and gives them policy guidance. It acts directly to build and maintain motorways and trunk roads in England, promotes road safety and undertakes transport research.

There are broadly similar responsibilities for Scotland and Wales, handled by the respective Secretaries of State.

Vehicle safety

Vehicles are regulated by legislation in the interests of safety and the environment. For example, construction and maintenance standards are laid down by law for cars and lorries, covering safety features such as collapsible steering wheels and seat belts; maximum noise levels and controls over exhausts and lead in petrol; minumum amount of tread on tyres; the MOT test for cars; and the heavy goods vehicle test for lorries.

Drivers of motor vehicles are licensed and tested to ensure minimum driving standards and these measures are backed up by legislation to curb dangerous driving, drinking and driving and excessive hours by drivers of lorries and coaches.

The Department's Driver and Vehicle Licensing Centre at Swansea handles the licensing of drivers in Great Britain, and the registration and licensing of vehicles throughout the United Kingdom.

Traffic management

Local authorities make the best use of roads through traffic management schemes. Though decisions are taken locally the regulations adopted conform to national standards set by the department.

These **traffic management schemes** aim to use road capacity effectively and to give priority to some types of movement over others. They are likely to contain a variety of measures. For example one-way streets, clearways and linked signals are all aimed at improving capacity, while bus lanes, pedestrian areas, cycle routes, parking controls and the restriction of access, restrain traffic and improve safety.

National roads

Motorways and **trunk roads** form a national network of major routes linking major centres of population, industrial areas, ports and airports. The cost of construction and repair is the responsibility of central government, but much of the actual work — including winter salting — is often carried out by local authorities as agents of the Secretary State.

However, the appraisal and design of new motorways and trunk roads is carried out by government departments, and most

94

major construction work is carried out by contractors directly appointed and supervised by them.

It may take many years before construction begins. Major roads and their structures cost millions and not only is there thorough economic assessment, but there has to be evaluation of various routes, taking into account environmental and social considerations.

The Department of the Environment is involved in road planning in England with final decisions taken jointly between the two ministers.

But before final decisions are taken, or indeed any routes designed in detail, various options are put out for the public, local councils and interested national and local organisations to give their views.

These consultation exercises nearly always involve exhibitions, press releases and public meetings. They provide a forum where various opposing factions can perhaps iron out their differences — freight hauliers versus environmentalists for example.

After this, a preferred route is decided upon, and it is then published in draft form, open to objection. This is a more formal stage and it is likely that a local public inquiry will be conducted by an inspector from the department. Recommendations will be decided jointly by two Secretaries of State — for Environment and Transport.

There is a right of appeal to the High Court on points of law, and there might possibly be further public inquiries if the minister has to adopt compulsory purchase powers to acquire the necessary land.

Local roads

Roads, other than those forming part of the national network of trunk roads and motorways administered by the department, are the responsibility of the metropolitan districts and the county councils; in Scotland, the regional or island councils.

These include a few short lengths of motorway usually occurring in urban areas, most 'A' roads, 'B' roads and all unclassified roads in rural and urban areas.

The resources for this new road building and the maintenance of existing roads come mainly from the local authorities' own resources aided by **Rate Support Grant**, but a contribution from central government is also made through **Transport Supplementary Grant** (TSG).

The decision on which road schemes take priority and the balance between how the TSG is issued, and how much local expenditure can be spent, is for the local authority to decide.

The local authority each year submits a **Transport Policy and Programme** (TPP) which is a comprehensive statement of policies with an expenditure programme. The appropriate minister then decides how much grant is to be handed out.

Road safety

Unsuitable roads contribute to accidents, and the likely reduction in casualties is taken into account when the department decides whether a trunk road improvement scheme is justified or not and whether its subsequent design should be approved.

Even small schemes, when carefully chosen, can produce significant reductions in the number of accidents and at a low cost. The department sponsors training courses, organised by the Royal Society for the Prevention of Accidents, for local authority engineers and road safety officers to help them identify schemes likely to give the best return for money spent.

Considerable care and research goes into the formulation of any safety measures or campaigns and every aspect of policy is examined. Much of the work of evaluating new suggestions for improving road safety is done by the experts of the Transport and Road Research Laboratory, but the framing of new laws and regulations, the consideration of their likely cost-effectiveness, whether they can be enforced and the assessment of whether they would command public support are the responsibility of the department.

Public transport

The present Government's aim of reducing state involvement has led to privatisation and the introduction of public capital into road and rail transport.

96

Bus operations in recent years have been deregulated and privatised, and competition is now allowed, but operators have to be licensed by **Traffic Commissioners** appointed by the department to oversee safety and quality of service.

An exception is London where, upon the demise of the Greater London Council, **London Regional Transport** was formed to take over buses and the underground, with an executive body appointed by the department.

The department has a more direct interest in railways which were nationalised in 1947 and are managed by the **British Railways Board**. The Government has sought to reduce the financial support and the board has had to improve efficiency and reduce costs to meet new financial targets. Since 1981 the board has sold off its hotels, shipping and hovercraft services to private enterprise.

Canals in some areas carry freight, and in others derelict stretches are being restored for leisure. Most canals are controlled by the publicly owned **British Waterways Board** which needs government grants to support its operations.

Shipping

The Department of Transport is responsible for most merchant shipping. While the present policy is minimum involvement and a concentration on free competition, the department does administer regulations for marine construction safety and welfare, and is responsible for preventing and cleaning up marine pollution.

Aircraft

The department is also responsible for a similar approach to air operations — promoting competition while ensuring high standards of safety. There are also international considerations involving agreements with foreign countries and the licensing of overseas operators flying into Britain, general airports policy, control of aircraft noise, aviation security policy and the investigation of accidents. The Secretary of State appoints members of the **Civil Aviation Authority (CAA)**, which is an independent statutory body generally responsible for the operational regulation of the industry, including air traffic control.

APPENDIX 1

THE TREASURY

A brief explanation of the various methods of revenue raising and the operation of the Budget. **(Not part of the syllabus.)**

The Treasury as an arm of government, is responsible for determining an overall economic policy for the United Kingdom. As a result, the department has a say in the policies of all departments of state in determining what level of services can be afforded.

The Budget

Governments have to raise taxes to finance their expenditure and this is done through the Budget. The budget takes place in March or April, though a government may always introduce further changes at other times of the year.

There are two main types of taxes:—

Direct Taxes — which are taxes on income and profit (e.g. income tax, corporation tax).

Indirect Taxes — which are taxes on sales (e.g. VAT, petrol tax and alcohol tax)

Most taxes, including indirect taxes, are permanent and remain in force until they are changed. The other taxes, including income tax, are annual and have to be reviewed and set annually.

The budget is enacted in the **Finance Bill** but unlike any other legislation, parts of the budget take effect before the Finance

Act is passed. Hence, some tax changes may come into force immediately — most commonly they will involve taxes on petrol, alcohol and cigarettes.

The Budget Process

Preparation for the budget takes many months and is accompanied by the publication of numerous financial statements and forecasts. In fact, the Treasury is required to publish two financial forecasts each year — one at the time of the budget and one in the autumn.

Recent budget speeches have tended to last around two hours. They contain detailed and technical statements, detailed changes to the taxation system, together with a general analysis of the economic policies of the Government.

Once the Chancellor of the Exchequer has made his speech, the budget resolutions are tabled to permit parts of the budget to take effect before the Finance Bill is approved. A six-day debate will follow and the Finance Bill is formally introduced. It will then follow the normal legislative procedure, though some parts of the committee stage will be taken on the floor of the House rather than in the committee. This is to permit more MPs to have a say.

The bill does go to the Lords but the powers of the Lords are severely limited by the Parliament Act 1911. The Finance Bill can receive the Royal Assent regardless of the Lords if they fail to pass it within a month. The Lords cannot amend the bill. The Finance Bill has to be passed by August 5.

Problems have occurred from time to time when changes brought in immediately after the Chancellor's speech were not passed by Parliament. When this happens the Government can be forced to amend the bill to make the changes temporary.

APPENDIX 2

COMMERCE AND THE STOCK EXCHANGE

A brief look at the types of companies and the function of the Stock Exchange. (**Not part of the syllabus.**)

The present Conservative Government, as explained earlier, is encouraging the expansion of the private sector, particularly the growth of small companies. In addition, the Government has adopted policies to encourage more individuals to own shares.

The terms public sector and private sector can confuse. The term **public sector** refers to that which is owned by the state and includes the nationalised industries. The **private sector** is concerned with ownership by private individuals. Puzzling to many is the fact that the private sector has both private and public companies!

There are four main types of business organisation:-

Sole trader

Most businesses are sole traders. For example, the corner shop, small garages, and the baker are all likely to be sole traders. The trader is solely responsible for his liabilities and if his business goes wrong he may have to sell his personal possessions to meet his debts.

This is known as unlimited liability. His business affairs are private and he is not required to disclose his accounts, except to the Inland Revenue, or to have them independently audited.

Partnerships

These are similar to sole traders but the profits and liabilities are shared by the partners. Many professionals (solicitors, accountants for example) set themselves up in partnership.

Private Limited Company (Ltd.)

These companies have a small number of shareholders who, should the company go bankrupt, are only liable for the share capital they own. Because of this limited liability for the debts, such companies are required to lodge certain information with the Registrar of Companies. The information they are required to give includes: directors' reports, names of directors, accounts etc.

Public Limited Company (Plc.)

These companies have made their shares available to the public by a full listing on the Stock Exchange. Entry to the Stock Exchange requires the disclosing of additional information.

THE STOCK EXCHANGE

The role of the Stock Exchange is to provide a market for those wishing to sell or buy shares. The price of the shares depends on the law of supply and demand. In other words, if there is a large demand for shares in one company their price will rise. The exchange finds a price at which a willing seller and a willing buyer will agree.

The term **Securities** is a general term which refers to stocks and shares. Basically, there are two types of securities. Firstly, those where the holder owns part of the company and secondly, those where he does not.

Equities or Ordinary Shares

With these the shareholders, between them, own the company and have a vote in how the company is run. They will also take part of the profit of the company, should the company make a profit, in the form of **dividends**. It is up to the directors to decide how much of the profits to give to the shareholders and how much to plough back into the company.

Gilts, Bonds, Loans, Debentures

Gilts are issued by the government and this is the main way in which the government borrows money. The government pays a fixed rate of interest on these for a fixed term and then repays the money to the holder. Bonds, loans and debentures are often issued by companies as well as by local authorities and public boards.

Stock Exchange Index

An index exists to measure the movement in prices of company shares. There are a number of them:—

F.T. Industrial Ordinary Share Index was started in 1935 and is based on a representative thirty British Companies.

All Share Index was started in 1962. Its name is misleading because it does not follow all British companies but is based on more than the first index.

F.T. 100 Share Index is based on the 100 largest companies.

BRITISH COMPANIES — INFORMATION SOURCES

There are a number of useful sources which journalists may use to find information on companies.

Companies Registration Office Directory
(Companies House, Cardiff).
All companies have by law to register and this register lists some 850,000 companies with their registered address, date of establishment and date of latest annual returns. Information is available by post.

Kelly's Manufacturers and Merchants Directory
(75,000 entries)

Sell's Directory of Products and Services
(60,000 entries)

Kompass Register of British Industry and Commerce
(30,000 entries)

Key British Enterprises
(20,000 entries)

It is worth remembering that the British Telecom Telex Directory contains 85,000 entries, which is more than any of the other directories.

APPENDIX 3

USEFUL INFORMATION SOURCES

Advisory, Conciliation and Arbitration Service
11-12 St. James's Square,   Tel: 071-210 3600
London, SW1Y 4LA

Agriculture, Fisheries and Food, Ministry of
3 Whitehall Place, London, SW1A 2HH   Tel: 071-270 8973

Arts Council of Great Britain
105 Piccadilly, London, W1V 0AU   Tel: 071-629 9495

British Council
10 Spring Gardens, London, SW1A 2BN   Tel: 071-930 8466

British Waterways Board
Melbury House, Melbury Terrace,   Tel: 071-262 6711
London, NW1 6JX

Buckingham Palace Press Office
Buckingham Palace, London, SW1A 1AA   Tel: 071-930 4832

Cabinet Office
Government Offices, Great George Street,   Tel: 071-270 6356
London, SW1P 3AQ

Charity Commission
St. Albans House, 57/60 Haymarket,   Tel: 071-210 4468
London, SW1Y 4QX

Civil Aviation Authority
CAA House, 45-59 Kingsway,   Tel: 071-379 7311
London, WC2B 6TE

Confederation of British Industry
Centre Point, 103 New Oxford St.,   Tel: 071-379 7400
London, WC1A 1DU

Customs and Excise, HM
King's Beam House, Mark Lace,   Tel: 071-626 1515
London, EC3R 7HE

Defence, Ministry of
Main Building, Whitehall,   Tel: 071-218 9000
London, SW1A 2HB

Education and Science, Dept. of
Elizabeth House, York Road,   Tel: 071-934 9884
London, SE1 7PH

Electricity Council
30 Millbank, London, SW1P 4RD   Tel: 071-834 2333

Employment, Dept. of
Caxton House, Tothill Street,   Tel: 071-213 7439
London, SW1H 9NF

Energy, Dept. of
Thames House South, Millbank,   Tel: 071-211 4545
London, SW1P 4QJ

Environment, Dept. of
2 Marsham Street, London, SW1P 3EB   Tel: 071-212 3434

European Communities, Commission of the (UK Office)
8 Storey's Gate, London, SW1P 3AT   Tel: 071-222 8122

European Parliament Information Office
2 Queen Anne's Gate, London, SW1H 9AA   Tel: 071-222 0411

Fair Trading, Office of
Field House, Breams Buildings,   Tel: 071-242 2858
London, EC4A 1PR

Foreign and Commonwealth Office
Downing Street (West), London, SW1A 2AL Tel: 071-270 3100

Health and Safety Executive
Baynards House, 1 Chepstow Place,   Tel: 071-229 3456
London, W2 4TF

Health and Social Security, Dept. of
Alexander Fleming House,   Tel: 071-403 5044
London, SE1 6BY

Health Service Commissioner (Ombudsman)
Church House, Great Smith Street,   Tel: 071-261 8445
London, SW1P 3BW

Home Office
Queen Anne's Gate, London, SW1 9AT   Tel: 071-213 3000

House of Commons
London, SW1A 0AA   Tel: 071-219 4272

House of Lords
London, SW1A 0PW   Tel: 071-219 3107

Information, Central Office of
Hercules Road, London, SE1 7DU   Tel: 071-928 2345

Manpower Services Commission
236 Gray's Inn Road, London, WC1X 9HL   Tel: 071-278 3222

Metropolitan Police
New Scotland Yard, Broadway,   Tel: 071-230 2171
London, SW1H 0BG

Nature Conservancy Council
Northminster House, Peterborough, PE1 1UA Tel: 0733 40345

Parliamentary Commissioner for Administration
(Ombudsman)   Tel: 071-261 8445
Church House, Great Smith Street, London, SW1P 3BW

Police Complaints Authority
10 Great George Street,   Tel: 071-261 8445
London, SW1P 3AE

The Post Office
Public Relations Dept., Post Office Headquarters,
33 Grosvenor Place, London, SW1X 1PX   Tel: 071-245 7443

Prime Minister's Office
10 Downing Street, London, SW1A 2AA   Tel: 071-930 4433

Sports Council
16 Upper Woburn Place,   Tel: 071-388 1277
London, WC1H 0QP

Trade and Industry, Dept. of
1 Victoria Street, London, SW1H 0ET   Tel: 071-215 7877

Trades Union Congress
Congress House, Gt. Russell Street,   Tel: 071-636 4030
London, WC1B 3LS

Transport, Dept. of
2 Marsham Street, London, SW1P 3EB   Tel: 071-212 0431

Treasury, HM
Information Division, Treasury Chambers,
Parliament Street, London, SW1P 3AG   Tel: 071-270 5238

Water Authorities Association
1 Queen Anne's Gate, London, SW1H 9BT   Tel: 071-222 8111

Welsh Office
Information Division, Cathays Park,   Tel: 0222 825111
Cardiff, CF1 3NQ

Additional telephone numbers for Government Departments and Public Corporations can be found in the Central Office of Information pamphlet, "Information, Press and Public Relations Officers"

USEFUL REFERENCE SOURCES

Britain — Official Handbook

Dodds — Parliamentary Companion

Whitakers Almanac

INDEX

111

113

114

Speaker of, 12, 27
Lords of Appeal, 26
Lords Spiritual, 26

MAT, 67
MEP, 53
MP, 17-26, 80, 100
MSC, 72-73
Magna Carta, 10
maladministration, 28, 64
Management Board, National
   Health Service, 62
manpower policy, 69, 72-75
Manpower Services Commission,
   membership, 72
   services,
      Job Training Grants, 71, 73
      Job Training Scheme, 73
      Youth Training Scheme,
      72-73
marine pollution, 90, 97
maternity pay, 67
May, Erskine, 11
Medical Appeal Tribunal, 67
Members of the European
   Parliament,
   election of, 53-54
   role of, 54
Members of Parliament,
   election of, 17, 47-50
   role of, 17-19, 19-26, 80, 100
metropolitan district councils, 93
Metropolitan Police, 58
Mines Inspectorate, 78
ministers,
   appointment of, 30, 31
   cabinet, 34
   convention of collective
      responsibility, 11, 34
   convention of individual
      ministerial responsibility, 35
   junior, 34
   non-cabinet, 34
   sponsoring, 80, 81
Minister of State, 34, 57, 61, 85
Minister of State for Health, 61
Minister of State for Social
   Services, 61
ministerial responsibility, 35
mobility allowance, 67
monarchy, 13-16, 57, 58, 60
   audience with Prime Minister,
      13
   Civil List, 16
   conventions concerning, 11
   payment of, 16

role of, 12, 13-16, 22, 29
Money Bill, 19, 23, 26
Montesquieu, 11
motorways, 93, 94-95

NHS, 62-66
NIREX, 91
National Advisory Committee for
   Telecommunications, 82
National Executive Committee,
   Labour Party, 42
National Health Service,
   ambulances, 64
   Commissioner, 64-65
   Community Health Council, 63
   complaints against, 64-65
   Department of Health and
      Social Security, 62
   District Health Authority,
      62-63
   Family Practitioner
      Committee, 63-64
   finance for, 62, 66
   general managers, 63
   Health Boards (Scotland), 64
   Health and Social Services
      Boards (N. Ireland), 64
   Health Service Commissioner,
      64-65
   joint consultative committee,
      65
   Local Health Council
      (Scotland), 64
   Management Board, 62
   ombudsman, 64-65
   organisation of,
      England, 62-64
      N. Ireland, 64
      Scotland, 64
      Wales, 64
   problems of, 65-66
   Primary Care Divisions
      (Scotland), 64
   private sector, 65
   Regional Health Authority, 62
   Supervisory Board, 62
National Insurance, 61, 66-67
   appeals, 67
   benefits, 61, 66-67
   finance of, 66
National Insurance Fund, 66
national parks, 90
National Radiological Protection
   Board, 91
national scenic areas (Scotland), 90
National Trust, 89

115

nationalised industries,
    boards of, 80
    control of, 80-81
    organisation of, 79-80
naturalisation, 57
Nature Conservancy Council, 90
New Years Honours List, 15
1922 Committee, 26, 30-31
Northern Ireland, 47, 62
Nuclear Industry Radioactive
    Waste Executive, 91
Nuclear Installations Inspectorate,
    78

OFGAS, 82
OFTEL, 82,
Office of Gas Supply, 82
Office of Telecommunications, 82
ombudsman,
    Commissioner for Complaints,
    65
    Health Service, 64-65
    Parliamentary, 28
Opposition, The,
    Leader of, 14, 20
    role of, 20
order in council, 22
ordinary closure, 24
ordinary shares, 102

PLC, 102
PSA, 91
pairing, 19
Parliament (see Commons and
    Lords)
Parliament Act 1911, 10, 14, 22,
    100
Parliament Act 1949, 10, 14, 22
Parliamentary Boundary
    Commission, 47, 54
parliamentary candidate, 50
Parliamentary Commissioner of
    Administration, 28
Parliamentary Labour Party, 26,
    31
Parliamentary Private Secretary,
    34, 36
parliamentary privilege, 20
parliamentary sovereignty, 12
Parliamentary Under Secretary,
    34, 57, 61, 85
parole, 58
partnerships, 102
partnership scheme, 71
party agents, 45
peers,

hereditary, 26, 27
life, 26
spiritual, 26
pensions,
    invalidity, 67
    retirement, 66
    war, 61
    widows, 66
Permanent Secretary, 36
planning, 87
planning inquiries, 88
police,
    authority, 59
    chief constable, 58, 59
    committee, 59
    Home Secretary, 58-59
    Metropolitan, 58
political parties,
    finance for, 45
    organisation of,
        Conservative, 39-41
        Labour, 41-43
        Liberal, 43-44
        Social Democratic, 44
    selection of candidates by,
        Conservative, 40
        Labour, 42
political sovereignty, 13
pollution control, 90-91, 97
Post Office Advisory Committees,
    81
postal vote, 49
Primary Care Divisions (Scotland),
    64
Prime Minister,
    appointment of, 11, 14, 29
    audience with the monarch, 13
    and the Cabinet, 31
    powers of, 15, 29-32
    question-time, 25
prisons, 58-59
private bills,
    definition of, 21
    passage of, 24
private limited companies, 102
Private Member's Bill,
    definition of, 21
    passage of, 25
Private Secretary, 36
private sector, 82, 83, 101
privatisation, 79
Privy Council,
    membership of, 14,
    role of, 14-15, 22
Professional and Executive List, 75
prohibition notice, 78

116

Property Services Agency, 91
prorogation, 14
prospective parliamentary
    candidate, 50
proxy vote, 49
public bills,
    definition of, 21
    passage of, 21-22
public corporations, 79-80
public inquiries, 87
Public Limited Companies, 102
public sector, 79-81, 101

QUANGO, 72
quasi autonomous non
    governmental organisation, 72
queen, 13-16, 57, 58, 60
    audience with Prime Minister,
        13
    Civil List, 16
    conventions concerning, 11
    payment of, 16
    role of, 12, 13-16, 22, 29
    speech of, 13
Queen's Speech, 13
question time,
    European Parliament, 54
    U.K. Parliament, 25, 80
quote scheme, disabled employees,
    77

RHA, 62
ROSPA, 96
race relations, 57
Race Relations Act 1968, 10
railways, 97
rate capping, 87
recreation, 85, 90
regional councils (Labour Party),
    41
regional health authority, 62
    chairmen of, 62
    finance for, 62
    general managers of, 63
    role of, 62
regional policy, 69-71
regional selective grants, 70
rent officers, 86
report stage, 21
reporters (Scotland), 88
Representation of the People Act
    1969, 10, 48
resignation honours list, 15
restart programme, 74
retirement pension, 66
returning officer, 50

roads,
    local roads, 95-96
    management of, 94
    motorways, 94-95
    planning and construction of,
        94-95
    road safety, 93, 96
    trunk roads, 94-95
road safety, 93, 96
Royal Assent, 22
Royal Family, 16
royal palaces, 89
royal pardon, 15, 58, 59
royal prerogative, 15
Royal Society for the Prevention of
    Accidents, 96
rule of law, 13

SSAT, 67
safety,
    at work, 69, 78
    roads, 93, 96
Safety at Work Act 1974, 78
Scotland, 36-37, 47, 58, 62, 85, 87,
    88, 89, 90, 93
Scottish Development Department,
    36, 89
Scottish Office, The, 36-37, 85
Scottish Standing Committee, 23
second reading, 21
Secretary of State,
    appointment by, 30, 31
    conventions concerning, 34-35
    role of, 34
Secretary of State for
    Employment, 72, 77, 78
Secretary of State for Energy, 80
Secretary of State for the
    Environment, 85-91, 95
Secretary of State for Health and
    Social Security, 61, 62
Secretary of State for Scotland, 36,
    58, 62, 93
Secretary of State for Trade and
    Industry 80
Secretary of State for Transport,
    95-97
Secretary of State for Wales, 37,
    47, 62, 64, 70, 85, 89, 93
securities, 102
select committee, 22, 23, 80
Sell's Directory of Products and
    Services, 103
separation of powers, 11, 12
shareholders, 79, 102
share indexes, 103

117